California Natural History Guides: 31

CALIFORNIA AMPHIBIANS AND REPTILES

BY
ROBERT C. STEBBINS

Illustrated by the author

UNIVERSITY OF CALIFORNIA PRESS
BERKELEY, LOS ANGELES, AND LONDON

UNIVERSITY OF CALIFORNIA PRESS
BERKELEY AND LOS ANGELES, CALIFORNIA
UNIVERSITY OF CALIFORNIA PRESS, LTD.
LONDON, ENGLAND

ISBN 0-520-02090-1
LIBRARY OF CONGRESS CATALOG CARD NUMBER: 72-165229
PRINTED IN THE UNITED STATES OF AMERICA

2 3 4 5 6 7 8 9 0

CONTENTS

Cover illustrations by Dr. Nathan W. Cohen:

Upper left: Collared Lizard
Lower left: Western Toad
Upper right: California Mountain Kingsnake
Lower right: Santa Cruz Long-toed Salamander

Recording observations in the field.

INTRODUCTION

If you enjoy amphibians and reptiles—salamanders, frogs, turtles, snakes, and lizards—California has much to offer. Its varied topography and climate provide living conditions for 123 species (including two established introduced forms) comprising one of the richest faunas of its kind anywhere in North America, but you must know where, when, and how to look to find them.

Although some reptiles and amphibians are easily seen by anyone who will search for them at the proper time of year, others may not be found unless one has special information about them. For example, you will probably not find a Tiger Salamander until you learn that they live in the grasslands and are seldom abroad except after heavy rains in winter, or find a Long-tailed Brush Lizard until you know they are found on the branches of the desert creosote bush. Some species are seldom seen even by scientists. The Western Black-headed Snake is an example. Persistent hunting in the proper habitat at the right season is required to find such a scarce animal. The main purpose of this book is to provide you with the information you will need to find and identify both the common and rare species, for it is through personal observation that you will obtain your greatest enjoyment and understanding of these animals. Don't be in too big a hurry to catch them. Watch them closely in their natural habitats. Some species will allow close approach. Others, more wary, can be observed quietly at a distance through field glasses to see how they behave when undisturbed. For a closer look, cage individuals for brief examination on the spot then let them go where found.

Disturbance of habitat and overcollecting is seriously threatening many of our wild species. If you feel you must have an amphibian or reptile for classroom study or as a pet, select a common one and find it yourself (this book will help you do so). Do not purchase it at a pet shop. When you are through with it, return it to the place of capture where it will have a chance to survive. An animal released in an area unfamiliar to it will usually soon die. Do not sell amphibians and reptiles, for you will be contributing to the demise of native species. Survival of these animals in pet shops is often poor, therefore many more must be procured than will be sold. As a consequence sales represent only a fraction of the total loss to the wild populations of these animals. Our wild animals cannot long withstand such impact, now spurred on by rapidly mounting demand as human population grows.

In addition to this book's main function as a field guide, special effort has been made to provide information that is frequently requested by youth groups and the general public—the truth about various snake "beliefs," facts on venomous snakes in the United States, and the like. This has required the inclusion of some information that applies to species outside of California.

Suggestions have also been made of things one can do with reptiles and amphibians to learn more about them. To illustrate, one can discover how a tadpole

Respiration of Bullfrog tadpole.

Ensatina in defense pose.

breathes by placing a drop of ink in the water in front of its mouth (illus.), and the defense reaction of an Ensatina can be set off by tapping it on the back (illus.) but might not be seen in ordinary handling.

If you are an alert, accurate observer, even though you have had no special training, you may make discoveries that will contribute to the advancement of the science of herpetology—the study of amphibians and reptiles.

For additional information consult my book, *A Field Guide to Western Reptiles and Amphibians,* 1966, Houghton Mifflin Company Boston, xiv + 279 pp.

ACKNOWLEDGMENTS

I am grateful to Dr. Robert Livezey and Dr. Bayard H. Brattstrom for their critical reading of the manuscript. The Houghton Mifflin Company gave permission for use of the following illustrations from my *Field Guide to Western Reptiles and Amphibians,* 1966: Plates 1(1), 2(2), 5(2), 6(3), 9(1), 12(2), 13(2), 23(2), 29(2), 30(2), 32(2), 33(1), 38(5); one Figure from front end paper. Numbers in parentheses are numbers of illustrations used from each plate. The McGraw-Hill

Book Company gave permission for use of the following drawings from my book *Amphibians and Reptiles of Western North America*, 1954: Plates 6E, 26A, 31 (top), 30D, 32C, 33, 34A–C, 39C, 40C, 41C, 41D, 64A, 68B and Figures 21, 22(14, 17, 18), 25(3), 26(2), 28(7, 10) 35(10–13). Numbers in parentheses refer to parts of figures. My wife, Anna-rose, rendered important assistance in typing the manuscript and aiding with editorial matters.

ACTIVITIES

Collecting and Studying

Amphibians and reptiles may be found by turning over rocks, logs, or other objects that serve as hiding places, but such objects should be replaced carefully so that the habitat is not disrupted. Many species can be caught by hand, but a reptile like the Western Fence Lizard may be elusive. To snare a lizard, attach a slip noose of fine copper wire (removed from an electric light cord), thread (number 40 or 50), nylon monofila-

Noosing a lizard.

ment, or fish line to the end of a pole and work the noose over the reptile's head. Approach slowly and avoid quick movements. On warm nights, snakes and some lizards may be found by driving slowly (15 to 20 miles an hour) along little-traveled, dark-paved roads where they may be seen on the pavement. Some lizards—the Desert Horned Lizard, Common Leopard Lizard, and others—can be found by watching for them on rocks along roadsides during morning hours when they are basking.

Looking for eyeshines of frogs.

Amphibian hunting in lowland and foothill areas is especially good after the first rains in the fall. By using a headlamp, you can detect the eye shine of toads, frogs, and other nocturnal animals whose presence might otherwise be overlooked. A flashlight held next to, and directed away from, your eyes will serve the same purpose. If you are driving, stop occasionally and shut off the motor in order to locate frogs by their voices. A kitchen strainer is useful for catching tadpoles or salamander larvae, and a dip net for catching frogs.

Reptiles can be carried in cloth sacks, but amphibians are better transported in jars containing damp moss, leaves, or a wet paper towel. Do not put a large amount of dirt with amphibians, as they may be crushed.

Note Taking

Your enjoyment in observing will be increased greatly if you gather facts about each animal and record your experiences. Every time you hunt for reptiles and amphibians, you are likely to obtain new information, and some of the things you see may be new to science.

When you record your observations, give the place, date, time of day, and your name (see p. 4). You can then describe the precise location, the kinds of plants present, character of the ground (sandy, rocky, amount of leaf litter and moisture, etc.), what the animal was doing, what other animals were present, and the weather conditions (temperature, etc.). To make a lasting record, use a loose-leaf notebook, a good grade of notebook paper, and permanent ink. Use a new page for each new species entry, heading the page with the name of the species, and add pages as necessary.

Continually strive for accuracy in taking notes. Do not draw conclusions hastily, but watch patiently, think carefully, and welcome repeated observations of the same animal. Avoid interpreting an animal's behavior in terms of your own—there may be great differences.

Amphibians and Reptiles as Pets

Although not appealing in the same way as a dog or cat, a pet lizard or frog can provide many interesting moments. Perhaps some people enjoy such animals chiefly because they are unusual or because of their attractive coloration and unexpected behavior. Some species are easily kept in captivity if provided with proper conditions. Examples are: the Western Fence

Lizard, the alligator lizards, Rubber Boa, Common Kingsnake, Red-legged Frog, Pacific Treefrog, Ensatina, and the newts.

In constructing a cage (terrarium) for your animal, a few essentials should be kept in mind. Good ventilation can be provided with a screen top. In attempting to get out, a snake may rub its nose raw on screening placed low on the sides of the box. At least one side should be glass to provide good illumination. A snugly fitting, removable tray in the bottom of the cage will aid cleaning. Use clean, dry sand, soil, or pea-sized gravel for reptiles or damp soil for amphibians. Rocks, pieces of bark, or boards may be used for a shelter. A water dish should be provided, a large one for turtles, frogs, or aquatic salamanders.

For reptiles a 75- or 100-watt electric light may be needed to warm the cage in cool weather to stimulate feeding and digestion. Adjust the heat so that there will always be a cool place where the air temperature does not go above 75° F. Contrary to popular belief, with but few exceptions, reptiles are not unusually tolerant of high temperatures. They will soon die, for example, if left in the sun on a hot day. Do not heat the terrarium for amphibians.

Captive reptiles may become dried out, especially if not feeding well. Sometimes a lizard or snake will drink if its nose is held under water for a moment. When swallowing movements begin, the reptile should be released.

Feeding your animal may prove to be your biggest problem. If your pet refuses to eat, it is best to release it and get another. Keep trying until you get one that eats well. A small quantity of food twice a week is usually ample for caged amphibians and reptiles. Do not leave a mouse or rat with a snake overnight. When the temperature falls, the reptile becomes sluggish and may be killed by its active, nocturnal "prey."

Termites found in rotting logs can be fed to frogs, lizards, and salamanders. Sometimes mealworms can be bought in pet shops for the same purpose. Insects, centipedes, spiders, sow bugs, earthworms, or other creatures caught in your garden or obtained on field trips may be used for pet food.

To keep tadpoles, put only one or two in a gallon of pond water, and change the water about twice a week. If tap water is used it should be allowed to stand exposed for a day or two. Feed them chicken mash, algae, rabbit pellets, egg yolks, bits of liver sausage, or lunchmeat. Do not allow uneaten food to rot and contaminate the water. As the tadpoles approach transformation, provide a rock or float for the small frogs to crawl onto.

MAJOR GROUPS OF AMPHIBIANS AND REPTILES

The frogs and toads, salamanders, and tropical caecilians are the major kinds of living amphibians. Salamanders resemble lizards but lack claws and have a moist skin without scales. Frogs (Anura, meaning "tailless") differ from salamanders in lacking a tail and in having hindlegs adapted for jumping. Caecilians are legless, wormlike or snakelike, and do not occur in the area covered by this book. Amphibian means "double-lived," and refers to the fact that many species dwell both on land and in water. Over 2,500 species are known. They range in size from the Little Grass Frog of southeastern United States, approximately ¼ inch in length, to the Giant Salmander of the Orient, approximately 6 feet long. In California, amphibians are represented by 25 kinds of salamanders and 20 frogs, all less than one foot in total length. The term "frog" is used here to cover all tailless amphibians, including toads, treefrogs, spadefoot toads, and so on.

In the United States, salamanders are most abundant in mountainous regions of the eastern part of the country, along the Pacific Coast and in the Cascade–Sierra Nevada mountain system. Except for the extreme northern part, no salamander has been found in the Great

Basin. The greatest number of species of toads is in the southwest and south, whereas treefrogs are most abundant in the southeast. The true frogs are somewhat more abundant in the eastern United States than in the west.

Turtles, lizards, snakes, and crocodilians are the four principal kinds of living reptiles. A fifth kind is represented by the 3-foot lizardlike Tuatara of New Zealand, the only survivor of a group of reptiles that lived 200 million years ago. During the "Age of Dinosaurs" that ended about 60 million years ago, many reptiles reached large size and became greatly varied in form and habits. The great dinosaur *Diplodocus* reached a length of 87 feet and weighed about 35 tons, and the batlike *Pteranodon,* with a wingspread of 22 feet, was the largest flying animal ever to have lived.

Today there are about 6,500 species of reptiles, but many of them are small and of secretive habits. The largest are the 33-foot Reticulated Python of southeast Asia and the 29-foot Anaconda of South America; the 10-foot Komodo Dragon, a giant lizard of the East Indies; the 8-foot Leatherback Turtle; and the 23-foot American Crocodile of tropical America.

In California, reptiles are represented by 33 species of snakes, the largest of which reaches approximately 7 feet; 36 lizards, the largest under 2 feet in total length; and 9 turtles, the largest, the marine leatherback, approximately 8 feet in length. This is about one-third of the total number of species inhabiting the United States.

In the continental United States there are some 116 species of snakes, 89 lizards, 38 turtles, and 2 crocodilians. The greatest number of lizards and snakes is found in the southern half of the United States where there are a wide variety of habitats and especially favorable temperatures. Most turtles are found in the eastern half of the country, only 7 species occurring west of the Rocky Mountains. The American Alligator inhabits southeastern United States, and the American Crocodile—distinguished from the alligator by its narrow head and more tapered, almost pointed snout—is found only at the tip of Florida.

In the United States there are only four types of dangerously venomous snakes: the copperhead, the water moccasin, rattlesnakes (15 species), and the coral snakes (2 species). In California, rattlesnakes (6 species) and the Gila Monster are the only dangerously venomous reptiles.

Amphibians

Amphibians are ectotherms, deriving their body temperature from their surroundings rather than from internal heat. When on land, they are often cooler than the environment because of the evaporation of water from the skin. Basking frogs, however, may be warmer than the air. The skin is smooth or warty, and usually well supplied with mucous and poison glands. The poison glands produce an acrid secretion that makes some amphibians distasteful and even poisonous to other animals. The secretion is irritating to human eyes.

The moist skin, mouth lining, and, in most species, lungs, function in respiration. Since these animals lack a watertight body covering, water passes freely through the skin. An amphibian will "dry up" if it does not have access to water, and, conversely, certain land-dwelling salamanders may become waterlogged and die if forced to stay in water. Skin permeability is not always a disadvantage in arid regions for a buried amphibian, such as a toad, can absorb moisture from the soil which is unavailable to other land vertebrates. Body water content is controlled by physiological mechanisms and by moving in and out of water and from moist to dry places on land.

At the time of breeding most amphibians travel over land to aquatic breeding places where mating takes place in the water. Most male frogs and toads form choruses and their voices attract other males and females to the breeding sites. The voice of each species is distinctive. The carrying qualities of the voice are often enhanced by balloon-like inflation of the throat which acts as a resonating chamber. This chamber is called the vocal sac. Some anuran males space out and set up calling stations from which they repel other males; voice and behavior may be used in maintaining territories (p. 86). When the females arrive they swim among the calling males and sexual encounters occur or the males actively search for females.

In mating the female is embraced (an act called "amplexus") by the male and sperm is released into the water surrounding the eggs as they are extruded. The embrace may be around the chest (pectoral) or around the waist (pelvic). Roughened dark patches of skin may appear at this time on one or more fingers of the male. They aid him in clinging to the slippery body of the female. His forelimbs may enlarge and become more

Red-legged Frogs in amplexus.

muscular and, in frogs, the base of the "thumb" becomes swollen. Fertilization is external (except in the Tailed Frog, p. 67), in the manner of most fish.

Salamanders, on the other hand, do not employ voice (with rare exceptions they are mute) in attracting the sexes but rely primarily on a little understood directional sense, probably involving celestial navigation and recognition of familiar environmental odors, in homing on breeding sites. Males may identify females by their odor as has been shown in newts. Most of our aquatic species engage in amplexus, the male riding "piggy-back" on the female and clasping her with his forelimbs about her chest. Afterwards the pair separates and the male deposits a spermatophore—a cone of jelly-like substance with a capsule of sperm at its top. The female

Courtship and mating of Ensatina.

crawls over the spermatophore and picks off the sperm capsule with the lips of her vent. The spermatozoa swim to a special chamber in the roof of her cloaca where they are stored and released to fertilize the eggs as they are laid. Fertilization is thus internal. In some of the more primitive salamanders, not found in California, spermatozoa are released over the eggs as in frogs.

Terrestrial, lungless salamanders, members of the family Plethodontidae, omit amplexus. Depending on the species, the male taps the head of the female with his snout, rubs her throat with his head or body (a, illus.), or scratches her with projecting upper jaw teeth. She applies her throat to his lower back or tail base and he leads her about with his back arched and tail trailing between or to one side of her legs (b). As the spermatophore is deposited he rocks from side to side or, in some species, rhythmically raises and lowers his hindquarters. The female may wag her head in counter fashion, stroking the lower back or tail base of the male. She then reapplies her throat and he leads her over the spermatophore. In Ensatina, as the female grasps the sperm capsule with her vent, the male lunges backward and strokes her body with his tail (c).

Most amphibian eggs are laid singly, in clusters, or in long strings, are pigmented on the upper side which faces the light, and are surrounded by one or more transparent jelly-like coats. The jelly protects the eggs against mechanical shock, brief periods of desiccation, disease organisms, and some kinds of predation. Eggs of lungless salamanders, which are deposited in dark places and go through full development to transformation on land, are large and unpigmented. Some of these salamanders are unusual in that they brood their eggs.

Most amphibians have an aquatic larva. The differences between tadpoles, the larvae of frogs and the larvae of salamanders can be seen in Figures 1 and 2, pp. 18 and 19. Our aquatic salamander larvae are of two types—pond and stream. The pond type lives in the

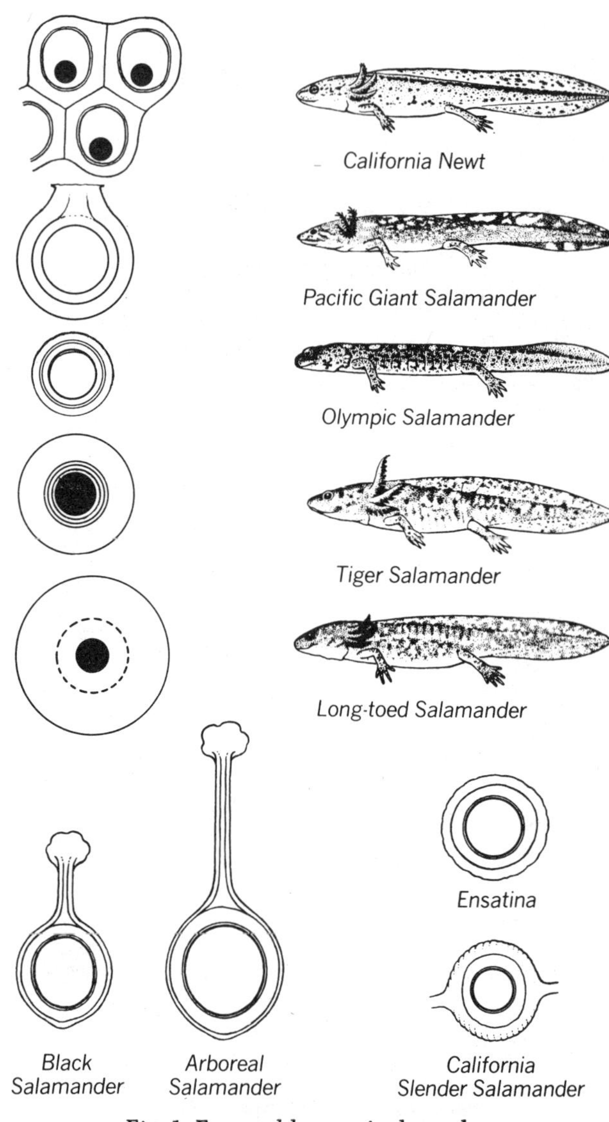

Fig. 1. Eggs and larvae of salamanders.

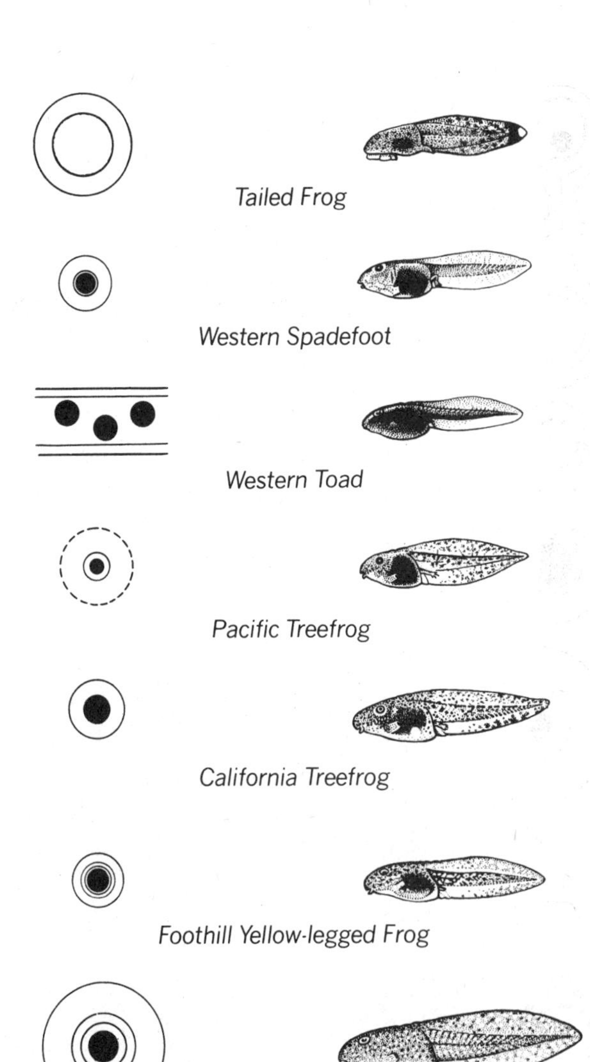

Fig. 2. Eggs and tadpoles of frogs.

quiet water of ponds, lakes, and the slower parts of streams, and usually has long feathery gills, a high dorsal fin that extends forward to near the back of the head, and long toes. Examples are the California Newt, Tiger, and Long-toed Salamanders. The stream type lives in brooks and streams and has short bushy gills (**Pacific Giant Salamander**) or, as in the Olympic Salamander, vestigial gills, the dorsal fin is reduced in length and height, usually extending little farther forward than the base of the tail, and the toes are generally shorter than in the pond type.

Gills are external and both forelimbs and hindlimbs develop externally in salamander larvae, whereas in tadpoles gills are internal (except at hatching) and the front legs develop concealed within the gill chambers until near the time for emergence on land. Water flows freely over the gills of salamander larvae but must be taken into the mouth, passed over the gills, and expelled

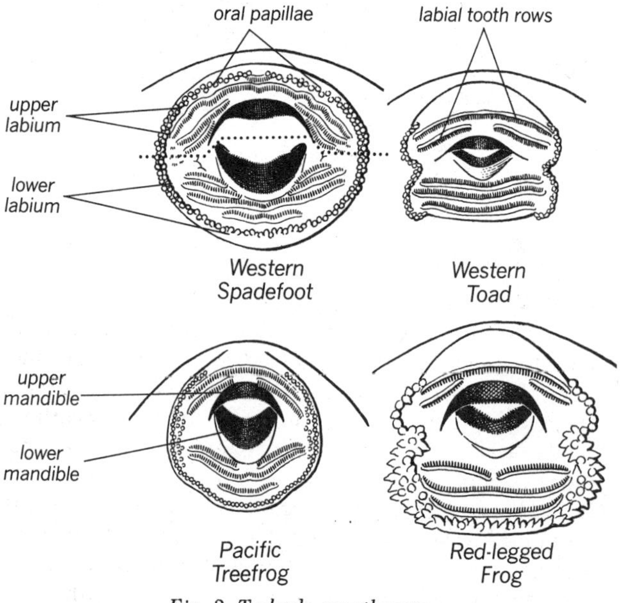

Fig. 3. Tadpole mouthparts.

through a small opening, the spiracle (usually located on the left side), in tadpoles.

Most tadpoles are herbivorous or scavenging and have horny mandibles and numerous comblike teeth arranged in transverse rows on their lips (or labia) with which they scrape small plants and decaying material from rocks and sticks in the water (Fig. 3). The labial tooth formula 2/3, 6/6, etc. indicates the number of rows, (a row broken at the midline is counted as one) on the upper and lower labia, respectively. Labial tooth counts are sometimes useful in identifying species. At the border of the mouth are oral papillae with which the tadpole perhaps feels and tastes food. A magnifying glass will be needed to see tadpole mouth parts. Salamander larvae are carnivorous and scavenging and have

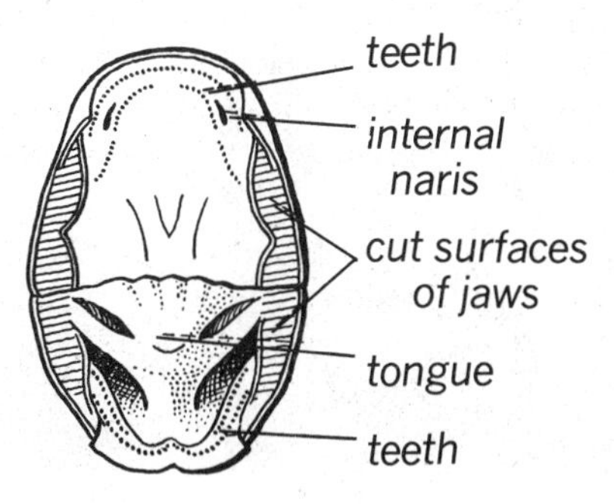

Fig. 4. Mouth of salamander larva.

small sharp true teeth. (Fig. 4)

The Western Spadefoot Toad illustrates an amphibian life cycle. Many jelly-coated eggs—sometimes more than 2,000 laid by a single female—are deposited in fresh water. They hatch into tadpoles that breathe by means of gills and that feed chiefly on plants, small animals, and decaying matter in the water. Later, the limbs appear, the gills are replaced by lungs, and the tadpole changes into a toad that, for a time, may retain a remnant of a tail. After a period of growth, the Spadefoot returns to water to breed. Not all amphibians go

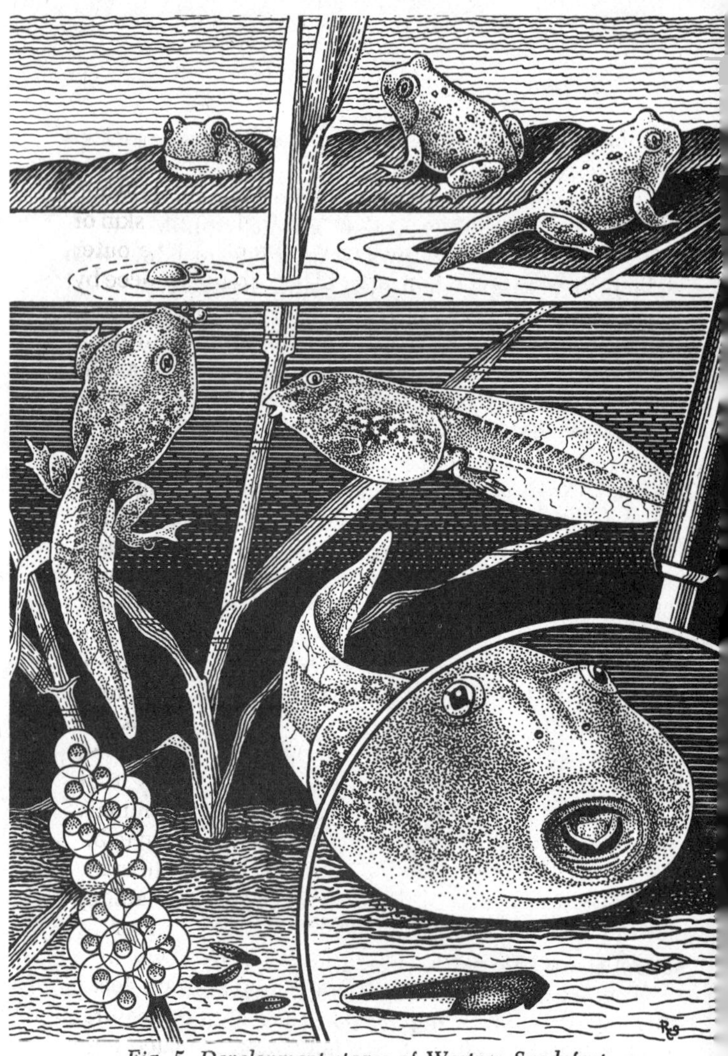

Fig. 5. Development stages of Western Spadefoot.

through such a cycle. Some lay their eggs on land and the young hatch fully formed, whereas others are completely aquatic. Between these extremes are a great array of species that show many fascinating specializations from frogs that carry their tadpoles in their vocal sacs or on their backs to those that defend their tadpole broods against the attack of predators.

Reptiles

Reptiles have scales and their skin is dry (except when they immerse), in contrast to the moist, glandular skin of amphibians. As growth and wear take place, the outer layer of the skin is shed, in large pieces or in one piece by snakes and some lizards. In snakes the old skin loosens around the mouth and is turned back, inside out, as it catches on sticks, rocks, and other rough surfaces as the snake crawls. Even the watchglasslike covering of the eye is shed along with the head skin.

Like amphibians and all other animals except birds and mammals, reptiles are ectothermic, deriving their body temperature chiefly from their surroundings. When their temperature is well below ours, they feel cold to us. Most of them, however, exercise control over their temperature by moving from sunlight to shade, from land to water, or in and out of the ground. In this way, many species are able to keep their temperature at a nearly constant level, and often well above air temperatures, during periods of activity. Some lizards, for example, can maintain their temperature at or above that of man. Consequently during most of the day, they may actually be as "warm-blooded" as many mammals.

Having a nearly impervious skin, reptiles have become widely distributed on land and have invaded even the driest parts of deserts where they are among the most successful animals. Most conserve water by releasing their urinary wastes in semisolid form as a small mass of whitish material attached to their feces. Some species are also able to tolerate high concentrations of wastes in their tissues and to accept such high levels until they are able to drink and reduce them by excretion. The Desert Tortoise stores water in its bladder, upon which it can draw when in need.

The major groups of reptiles in California are easily recognized. Turtles have a shell into which they can withdraw the head, tail, and limbs, Lizards differ from snakes in usually having limbs (the legless lizard is an exception), and their toes are provided with claws, a characteristic differentiating them from salamanders. No snake has movable eyelids, and thus the presence of eyelids will distinguish our legless lizard from a snake.

Fertilization of the eggs in reptiles occurs within the reproductive tract of the female and sperm is introduced by copulation. In some species the sperm is stored by the female making possible fertilization of eggs months or even years following copulation. In both lizards and snakes the copulatory organs (hemipenes) are paired structures inverted into the base of the tail. They can be extruded in a breeding lizard by gentle pressure on the underside of the tail, exerted from behind the swollen tail base toward the vent. They emerge as pinkish finger-like projections. Whitish masses of sperm may be present. When pressure is released the organs retract by turning in on themselves. Most breeding male lizards can be readily sexed by the swollen appearance of the tail. To determine the sex of a snake, gently probe the rear surface of the vent, toward the sides, with a slender blunt stick. In males the probe should extend deeply into the tail base as it passes into the hollow of the hemipenis. Male snakes generally have longer tails than females and their tails are broader at the base. Since the male reptile rests on the back or to one side of the female during copulation, paired organs permit him to reach her vent from either side of her body. Usually only one hemipenis is used in copulation.

With the exception of marine turtles, reptiles do not migrate to breeding sites. Most are highly territorial and adult males defend selected areas against other males but accept one or more females and often subordinate males in their midst. Adult females of some species also may be territorial. Male lizards defend their territories by ritualistic movements and displays and occasionally by fighting. The behavior pattern varies with different species but often the members of a taxonomic group (even an entire family) may have features in common. Many iguanid lizards (members of the large family Iguanidae) in California, for example, behave as follows: They bob their heads, sometimes flexing the forelimbs in "push-up" fashion, flatten their sides, and lower their throat skin, often displaying bright markings that are otherwise often concealed. Display alone may drive off a rival, but if the intrusion continues, a fight may occur. The combatants "face off," with bodies parallel and heads often in opposite directions. They strike with flattened sides and tail and may at times attempt to bite and "throw" their opponent. These battles seldom end in serious injury. A defeated lizard cowers (lies flat) or runs away. Male snakes, rattlers for example, may rear up and intertwine the anterior part of their bodies and attempt to "throw" one another to the ground. Tortoises may charge and strike with the heavy gular projections at the front of their shells, pulling their heads in just in time to avoid damage. You can sometimes witness territorial behavior in lizards if you tether a male about the waist on a 6-foot length of string and place him near another male. Attach the tether to a slender pole for ease in handling.

In the presence of a female the demeanor of the territorial male changes. Courtship in male iguanid lizards often involves "push-ups," and rapid vertical vibration of the head as the male approaches the female. In mating, he often seizes her by the skin of her neck or back and curls his hindquarters against her tail base. One leg may be placed across her lower back. Male alligator lizards hold the head of the female in their jaws.

Female iguanids that have copulated, often reject males by assuming a characteristic posture. They stand high, arch the back, flatten the sides, elevate the tail, and turn their hindquarters toward the male, perhaps releasing a repellent odor. In some species bright colors develop that may act as a further deterrent. A female heavy with eggs might sustain injury to herself or her eggs if copulation occurred at this time.

Mating in alligator lizards.

Male snakes often move the head in jerky lateral movements as they crawl along the back and sides of the female. The body is thrown into lateral undulations and the neck and sometimes loops of the body are moved in a massaging action across the back of the female. The tails of the pair may intertwine as the male brings his vent into position. If receptive the female opens her vent to receive the hemipenis. Odor is important in the sexual behavior of many snakes, and aids males in tracking and identifying females.

The mechanism used by snakes in finding their mates appears to be the same as that used by many reptiles in finding and testing food and in detecting enemies. The flicking tongue, moist and frequently protruded, picks up odor (or taste?) particles in the air or on the ground and transports them to two small sensory chambers in the roof of the mouth—the Jacobson's Organs. If a rattlesnake's mouth is taped so that it cannot protrude its tongue, it no longer gives its characteristic fear response in the presence of a kingsnake even though the kingsnake is in full view. This response consists of placing the head and neck against the ground, elevating loops of the body, and suddenly thrashing when touched.

Mating in turtles often includes circling and head bobbing by the male, lunges at the female resembling territorial defense, and, in some aquatic turtles, stroking of her head and neck with the elongate claws on his front feet as he circles in front of her. Mounting is from the rear and in many turtles a concavity on the underside of the male's shell accommodates the rounded back of the female and aids him in maintaining his position. The vent of the male is situated well out on the tail beyond the shell margin when the tail is held straight. This gives the leeway necessary to bring the vent against that of the female's when he curls his tail under hers to achieve union. The single copulatory organ lies inside the vent and is extruded at the time of copulation. The underside of the shell of females is usually flat or convex and the vent is situated toward the base of the tail, inside the shell margin.

Reptiles lay their eggs on land in pits dug in the soil, in rotting leaf litter or logs, and in crevices and other protected sites. The eggs usually have a white, flexible, almost leathery shell. The Desert Tortoise, however, lays eggs the size of ping-pong balls with a hard white shell. Soft-shell eggs swell as they absorb water from their surroundings, and the shell becomes taut. Rate of development varies with temperature. The young

Captive Coast Horned Lizard laying eggs. Under natural conditions the eggs are buried.

emerge fully formed and there is usually no parental care. Some reptiles are live-bearing and in the species descriptions such species are noted. Assume egg-laying unless otherwise indicated.

To rear reptile eggs place damp (not wet) soil in the bottom of a plastic bag, flatten out the soil, make a dent for each egg so they will not touch, catch some air in the bag and close the top with a rubber band. Keep at room temperature. Measure changes in egg size through the bag without opening it. Keep track of temperature and dates of laying and hatching.

SNAKES

Although the very old and widespread fear of snakes is declining, there are still many people who fear them. Fear of snakes dies hard. Big snakes and venomous snakes, throughout a long evolutionary past, have been a threat to primates, including man. Perhaps the distinctive snake form evokes alarm. Knowledge and understanding of these creatures readily dispels fear, however, especially if sought early in life, and great enjoyment can come from the study of these interesting animals.

Fear stimulates the imagination and there are few animals that have given rise to more false tales than snakes. These gentle reptiles have been endowed by gullible people with all kinds of remarkable powers, most of which are in some way threatening. Following are some examples of such folklore.

The "hoop snake" is said to take its tail in its mouth and roll down hill. Upon gaining momentum, it reputedly straightens out lancelike, and pierces its victim with a sharp spine at the tip of its tail. (Applied to the Racer, Whipsnakes, and the Mud and Rainbow Snakes of eastern United States.)

The "glass snake," actually a lizard *(Ophisaurus)*, has a long fragile tail which breaks into pieces when seized. A new tail is grown. There are three species in central and eastern United States and others elsewhere in the world

Although the story is widely believed, snakes cannot charm people or other animals. A bird or squirrel may watch a snake closely, recognizing it as a possible predator, but is not held spellbound.

Snakes are widely believed to chase people. Occasionally racers, including the Coachwhip, (p. 118) attack when cornered and the Black Mamba of Africa, the Tiger Snake of Australia, and a few others are sometimes aggressive, but most snakes try to get away when man comes near. Sometimes in hot weather a snake caught in the open may seek a person's shadow to avoid heat, giving an impression of attack.

Few snakes can jump, although jumping snakes are often reported by uncritical observers. When on level ground those that coil to strike are able to lash out a distance of about one-third their total length. On a hillside, they may do better. Rarely, an excited snake, especially a young one, may strike with such force as to leave the ground slightly. Certain South American vipers can actually leap a short distance, but, in general, snakes are unable to jump.

Snakes do not have to coil to bite.

A snake's tongue is not a stinger. The flickering tongue aids the snake in testing the chemistry of its environment as described on p. 26.

A female snake will not swallow her young to protect them. "Mother" snakes usually have no interest in their young. This story arises from the occasional discovery of a pregnant, live-bearing female with her body torn open and young still alive and ready for birth.

Snakes don't milk cows. Although they drink it is doubtful if they could effectively milk a cow, even if she were to tolerate the sharp teeth. Snakes do, however, enter barns and pastures to forage on rodents. (Applied to the Milk Snake, a species of Kingsnake, of eastern and central United States.)

A horsehair rope around one's sleeping bag is no protection against rattlesnakes. It is thought that the hairs of the rope annoy the snakes, but experiments have shown that they crawl over such ropes with impunity.

Rattlesnakes and bullsnakes are said to interbreed producing a dangerous hybrid called the "bullrattler." Since rattlers kill with venom and bullsnakes by constriction, the hypothetical hybrid has the option of poisoning or squeezing its victim to death. Bullsnakes (another name for gophersnakes) when alarmed often flatten and spread the head, hiss, and vibrate the tail, putting on an impressive display. In dry leaves a rattlesnake-like sound may be produced by the vibrating tail. Such behavior may have given rise to this false story.

There are reports of rattleless rattlesnakes in California. They have been given credence by the discovery, on Catalina Island in the Gulf of California, of a naturally occurring population of such rattlers. The reports are based on gophersnakes engaged in threat display.

Reports of "horned" snakes may be based on the sidewinder, a rattler that has projecting hornlike scales over its eyes, or frog-eating snakes such as gartersnakes, or the California Striped Racer seen with the legs of a frog protruding from its mouth.

These are just a few of the many misleading ideas about snakes. They are interesting as folklore, but the truth about snakes is far more worthwhile.

The danger from snakes in the United States is slight. In contrast to a country like Australia where about half the species are venomous, only 1 in 19 is dangerously venomous in our country. Everytime we cross a street or ride in an automobile we are in far greater danger than when we are on foot in snake country. Venomous snakes in the United States kill, on the average, 14 persons a year. They are less dangerous than lightning. The dangerously venomous snakes of the United States are the coral snakes (2 species), the Copperhead, the Water Moccasin, and the rattlesnakes (15 species). The coral snakes are relatives of the cobras and, like them, have erect, nonmovable, hollow fangs in the front of the upper jaw. Their venom acts chiefly on the nervous system, causing paralysis and interference with respiration and heart action. They are slender snakes with the head only slightly broader than the neck, no facial pits, and they lay eggs.

The Eastern Coral Snake ranges from North Carolina to southern Texas and to the tip of Florida. Its close relative, the Sonoran Coral Snake, is found from southern Arizona and southwestern New Mexico to southern Sonora, Mexico. It ranges to within a few miles of California and should be sought in some of our southeastern desert mountain ranges. The color pattern consists of alternating red and black bands separated by yellowish to whitish narrow bands. These are secretive, burrowing snakes that feed on other snakes and lizards. Our Western Shovel-nosed Snake and the Mountain Kingsnake resemble the coral snakes in color but they are harmless.

The remaining venomous snakes are "pit vipers." They give birth to their young, have a heat-sensitive pit on each side of the face between the eye and nostril (p. 133), a broad head set off from the slender neck, and movable hollow fangs used in injecting venom. The venom of most species acts on the circulatory system of the victim, breaking down the blood cells and walls of the blood vessels. Some, however, such as the Mojave Rattlesnake, have a strong neurotoxic component in their venom.

The Copperhead ranges from Massachusetts to western Texas and from southern Iowa to the Gulf Coast. The common name refers appropriately to the head color; the body is usually marked with dumbbell-shaped, chestnut-colored bands on a gray or brownish background. It is a woodland species that feeds on mice, birds, frogs, and insects. Fatalities from its bite are rare.

The Water Moccasin occurs from southeastern Virginia to southern Texas and from southern Illinois to the tip of Florida. When young, it resembles the Copperhead, which usually has a well-defined pattern, but the pattern becomes less definite with age, and large Water Moccasins may be blackish or dark olive. The lining of the mouth is white, which has given rise to the common name—"Cottonmouth." It is chiefly aquatic, and feeds on fish, frogs, lizards, snakes, birds, and small mammals. Large, heavy-bodied individuals of the Western Aquatic Garter Snake of the San Joaquin Valley, California, are sometimes mistaken for Moccasins, but they are harmless.

The rattlesnakes are widely distributed. At least one species is found in every state except Alaska, Hawaii, and the District of Columbia.

TREATMENT OF VENOMOUS SNAKE BITE

The only dangerously venomous snakes in California are the rattlesnakes of which there are six species. The Western Rattlesnake *(Crotalus viridis)* is most likely to be encountered because of its wide distribution and occurrence near centers of population. All other species, with the exception of the Red Diamond Rattlesnake *(Crotalus ruber)* of southern California, are found in the desert or its fringes. Of these desert forms, the Mojave Rattler has an especially potent venom that has a stronger effect on the nervous system than the others. Handling rattlesnakes is like playing with a loaded gun and should be avoided.

Although a rattlesnake is easily recognized, occasionally a person is bitten who neither sees nor hears the snake. (Rattlesnakes do always rattle before striking). It is important, therefore, to make sure that venom has been injected and that the bite was not that of a harmless snake before risking incision of the bite wounds. Other first-aid measures (see below) can be carried out while making this determination. If venom has been injected, pain is usually prompt and intense and swelling appears within about five minutes. The fang punctures can usually be found, but the teeth of a harmless snake can sometimes leave marks that look like those made by fangs. The snake should be sought and killed so that the carcass can be brought in for identification, important in prescribing treatment.

Unfortunately, complete agreement on the first-aid treatment for rattlesnake bite is lacking. The following is based chiefly on the recommendations of Dr. Findlay Russell, School of Medicine, University of Southern California (see *Cyclopedia of Medicine, Surgery, and Specialties*, ed. G. M. Piersol, 1962).

(1) If the mouth is free from cuts or sores, immediately suck the site of the bite while preparing for other first-aid measures.

(2) If a doctor can be reached in 15 or 20 minutes apply an ice pack to the bitten area and leave the rest of the treatment to him. If bitten on the finger or hand remove any rings or bracelets, for swelling may make their removal difficult later on.

(3) If a longer time is required for medical help, apply a constricting band around the extremity and cut open the fang punctures. Place the band above the wound, above the first joint near the injury. The band should impede the movement of venous blood and lymph, but should not stop arterial flow. The pulse should be felt beyond it. Much of the venom is carried in lymph channels that lie just beneath the skin. Loosen the band every 10 to 15 minutes for 90 seconds.

(4) Unless the wound is already bleeding freely, incise each fang puncture. Disinfect a sharp knife and the area of the bite. A match flame can be used on the former, but don't wipe off the soot or touch the cutting surface. Make a single straight incision ⅛ to ¼" long through each fang puncture at right angles to a line connecting them. The length of the cuts should not be greater than the diameter of the suction apparatus. Depth of the incisions should be approximately ½ the distance between the fang punctures. In cutting, take into account the direction of the strike and fang curva-

ture. The fangs curve toward the rear of the snake's mouth. The greatest concentration of venom usually lies slightly behind each puncture mark. Cut with great care to avoid tendons and larger blood vessels. Make no additional incisions.

(5) Apply suction by mouth if no mechanical devices are available. Suction should be *gentle* and maintained throughout the first hour following the bite.

(6) Place the injured part in an ice bath but keep the wound dry. Release the constricting band. Remove the part from the bath after one hour, but continue keeping it cool (around 10–15°C). Ice bags may be used. Under no circumstances should the injured member be kept in ice water for longer than one or two hours.

(7) Reassure victim. Although rattlesnake bite should be regarded with due concern, its danger must not be exaggerated. Among persons given proper treatment, on the average, less than 1 percent die. Do not allow the patient to become chilled. Immobilize the bitten part and keep the patient in a reclining position so far as possible.

All remaining procedures should be carried out by a physician. He may use antivenin to counteract the effect of the venom and antitetanus and antibiotics to control infection. His treatment will depend on the assessment of many variables—the victim's temperament, sensitivity to antivenin, the site of the bite, species of snake, and specific symptoms the patient shows.

CONSERVATION

Reptiles and amphibians, like all animals, are beset by many dangers, but the 9,000 species living today are proof that they have been successful in coping with problems of survival for thousands of years. Now, however, all wild animals face a grave new threat—the destruction of their habitats by man as a result of the explosive growth of his population, mounting pollution, and the use of modern technology to modify the earth's environments. These forces pose serious problems for man himself and bring changes to which many species of plants and animals cannot adjust. Every dam, freeway, subdivision, and farm that intrudes into wild lands causes damage to the living fabric that existed long before we came. Many "pest" control methods (mosquito and crop and forest pest abatement) inadvertently destroy beneficial animals. This is why those who are concerned about the protection of wildlife feel so strongly that population growth and the exploitation of nature must be restrained and that man must broaden his moral code to include respect for all life, not just those species that are considered beneficial to him. Unless we change our ways the list of extinct and nearly extinct species will continue to grow. All who care about man's future and that of other organisms must work to solve the problem of population growth and its accompanying destructive effects. On a smaller scale, the following should be kept in mind:

1. Do not collect rare or endangered species (see following section).
2. In obtaining animals for study, treat the habitat with great care and restore it by replacing rocks, logs, and other objects overturned in the search.
3. If you use a motorcycle or other off-road vehicle, stay on trails to prevent soil erosion and damage to plants and ground-dwelling animals. Walk slowly through areas of study. You will see more that way.
4. Seek to obtain and give accurate information in order to combat falsehood, superstition, and fear.
5. Kill no living thing wantonly.

RARE AND ENDANGERED SPECIES OF AMPHIBIANS AND REPTILES IN CALIFORNIA

In 1971 the State of California accorded legislative protection to 13 species and subspecies of amphibians and reptiles in California. This action was taken because of the small size of some of their populations, increasing habitat destruction, and removal of individuals by collectors. Species classed as *endangered* are considered to be nearing extinction; those classified as *rare* are to be watched closely for evidence of population decline. The latter may be reclassified as endangered at any time. Killing, collecting, or having in one's possession a *rare* or *endangered* animal without a permit is punishable by heavy fine and/or imprisonment.

The following are on the protected list:

Endangered

Desert Slender Salamander *(Batrachoseps aridus)*

Santa Cruz Long-toed Salamander *(Ambystoma macrodactylum croceum)*

Blunt-nosed Leopard Lizard *(Crotaphytus silus)*

San Francisco Garter Snake *(Thamnophis sirtalis tetrataenia)*

Rare

Kern Canyon Slender Salamander *(Batrachoseps simatus)*

Tehachapi Slender Salamander *(B. stebbinsi)*

Limestone Salamander *(Hydromantes brunus)*

Shasta Salamander *(H. shastae)*

Siskiyou Mountain Salamander *(Plethodon stormi)*

Black Toad *(Bufo boreas exsul)*

Southern Rubber Boa *(Charina bottae umbratica)*

Alameda Striped Racer *(Masticophis lateralis euryxanthus)*

Giant Garter Snake *(Thamnophis couchi gigas)*

In addition to the above species and subspecies the Desert Tortoise *(Gopherus agassizi)*, although not yet classed as rare or endangered, is given special legislative protection because of its vulnerability to vandals, disturbances of its desert habitat, low rate of natural replacement, and popularity as a pet. Killing, collecting, or possessing, without permit, a Desert Tortoise is also punishable by fine and/or imprisonment.

DESCRIPTIONS OF SPECIES

Information given in the descriptions of the various species is restricted to California and should not be considered as applying to the species as a whole. For more complete coverage, consult my *Field Guide to Western Reptiles and Amphibians* (Houghton Mifflin Co., 1966).

Identification. Only the more important species characteristics are given. These and the illustrations should suffice in making identifications. Measurements at the beginning of each description are in inches and give the approximate range in snout-vent length in salamanders, frogs and toads, and lizards; total length in snakes; and shell length in turtles. See Figures 6 and 7, pp. 38 and 39, illustrating technical terms not explained in the text. Characteristics that apply to two or more related species are covered in general sections and are not repeated in the descriptions. Always read these sections in obtaining information on the species in question.

Time of Activity. The usual time for amphibians in the lowlands and foothills is from the first rains in the fall—October or November—to the time of drying of the ground in spring—late April to June. At higher elevations and northward in the State activity begins after the snow melts and ceases with drying in late summer or fall or with the onset of cold weather. Hibernation occurs in winter. Along the lower Colorado River, in desert mountains, and in the Cascade–Sierran mountain system, activity may be stimulated by occasional summer showers. Cold or dry spells, even during peak periods, may cause reduction or cessation of activity.

Reptiles are usually active from March to October with a peak in April to July when most breeding occurs. Numbers increase in late summer and fall with the emergence of the season's young. As with amphibians inactivity occurs during cold or hot dry periods. Reptiles are more sensitive to cold than amphibians and more tolerant of dryness and heat.

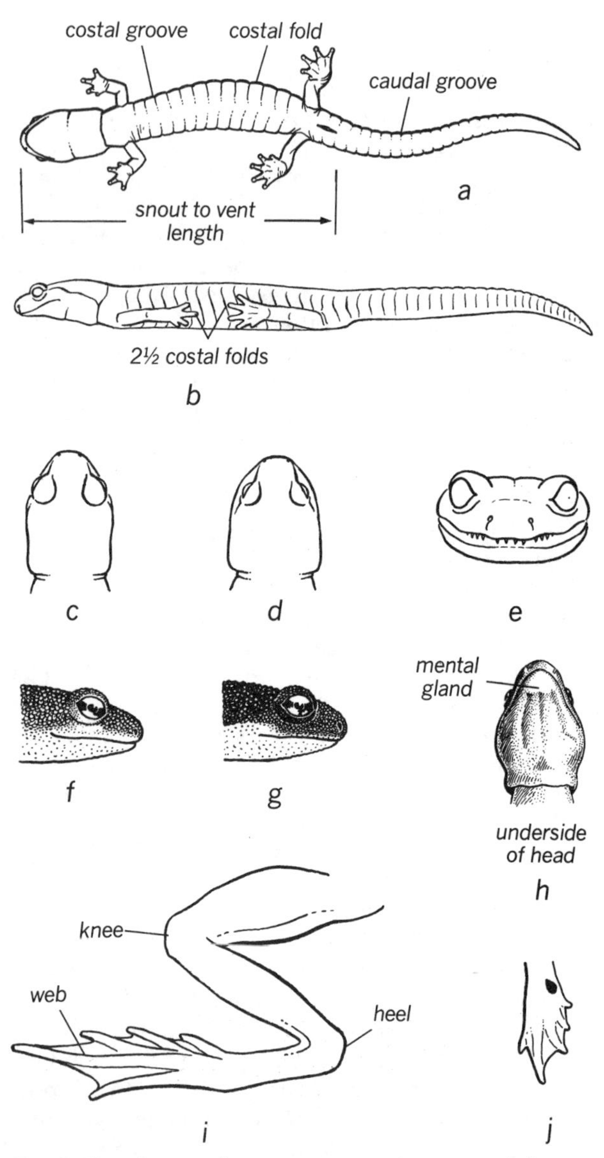

Fig. 6. Identification characteristics of California amphibians.

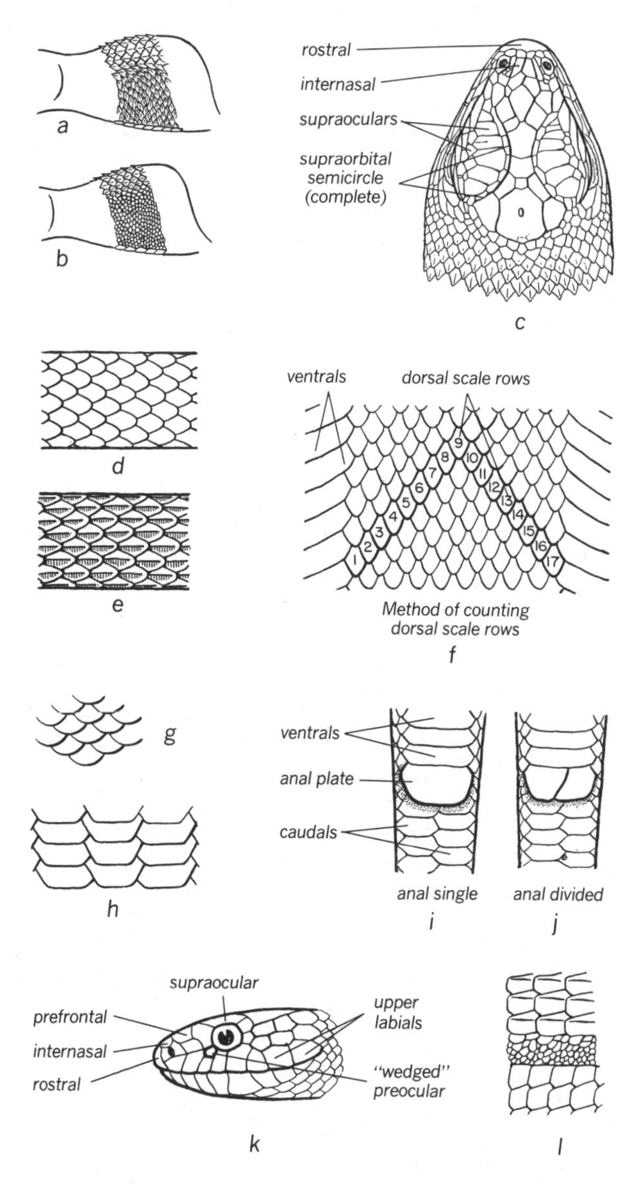

Fig. 7. Identification characteristics of California reptiles.

Assume the species to be diurnal unless otherwise stated. With the exception of the newts, and, occasionally the Pacific Giant Salamander, our salamanders are nocturnal or crepuscular (active at twilight). Frogs and toads are generally nocturnal, but daytime activity may occur in some species. especially at the height of breeding.

Many of our reptiles are diurnal but some are strictly nocturnal and others become crepuscular or nocturnal with the onset of hot weather. A few nocturnal species become diurnal during cool weather. Time of activity is to a considerable extent temperature dependent and varies with season and latitude. In a given species activity may start later and end earlier at high altitude and to the north than at low altitude and to the south.

Food. Amphibians eat a great variety of insects and other small animals, exercising little selection in their choice of food. Although some scavenging occurs, most will not feed unless they detect movements of their prey. They move within close range, focus intently with both eyes, and usually suddenly thrust out the tongue, catching the prey on its sticky tip. The prey is crushed with the jaws and promptly swallowed. Movements of the eyeballs may aid swallowing as these firm structures bulge downward and press against the food. Watch for eye movements as swallowing begins.

Reptiles are generally more selective in diet than amphibians. Most lizards feed on insects and other small animals but some feed almost exclusively on plants (are herbivorous), and some eat both plants and animals (are omnivorous), but usually the latter predominate in the diet. Snakes feed only on animals and their eggs. Turtles usually eat both plants and animals, but the tortoises are almost exclusively herbivorous.

Lizards seize food in their jaws and crush it or occasionally swallow it whole. The tongue is used to move the food about to aid in crushing and swallowing. Occasionally small items are caught by quick protrusion of the sticky tongue. Horned lizards may catch ants in this manner. Snakes kill their prey in several ways. They may simply seize it in their jaws and engulf it. This action may be aided by throwing loops of the body over the prey to impede its struggles (racers, gartersnakes). They may kill their prey with constriction, by encircling it with loops of the body and squeezing it to death (boas, Gophersnake, kingsnakes). They may kill with venom injected with hollow fangs or grooved teeth (rattlers, lyre snakes, Night Snake). Sharp, backward-pointing teeth in both upper and lower jaws provide most snakes with a sure grip. Great flexibility in the jaws makes it possible for them to swallow objects bigger around then they are.

The lists of foods given in the descriptions are not complete, but they will serve to indicate the kinds of foods taken by each species.

Range. The range and altitudes given apply only to California. For full information on range consult my field guide (see p. 7). Refer to the map, p. 42, to locate the geographic areas mentioned in the accounts. For example, "The desert" is interpreted broadly and includes the entire area east of the Cascade–Sierran mountain system and the Peninsular Ranges in southern California.

Amphibians

SALAMANDERS

Ambystomids (Family Ambystomidae)

Most are large heavy-bodied, smooth-skinned, and small-eyed, salamanders with flat-sided tail and a row of teeth across roof of mouth; costal grooves usually distinct. They spend most of their time on land, underground in burrows of ground squirrels, gophers, badgers, and other animals or within decayed logs or stumps. Abroad at night, usually only for brief periods during or following rains. In winter and early spring they often

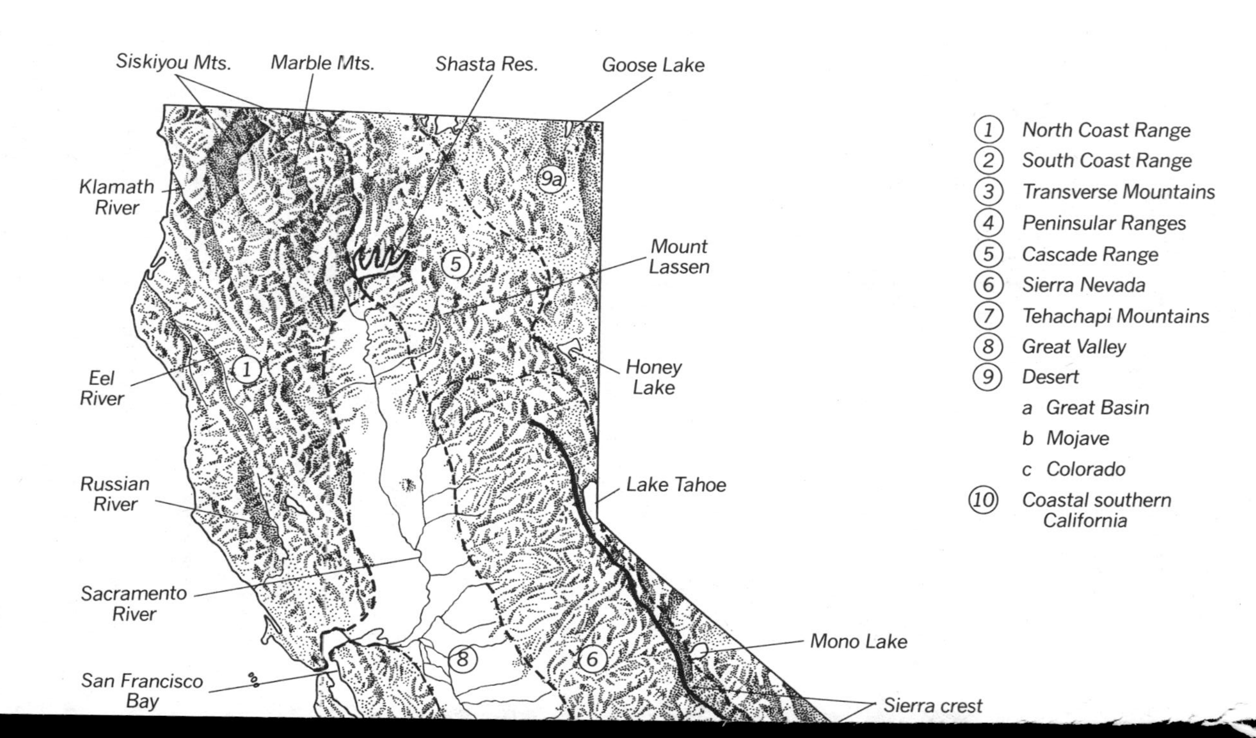
Siskiyou Mts.
Marble Mts.
Shasta Res.
Goose Lake
Klamath River
Mount Lassen
Eel River
Honey Lake
Russian River
Lake Tahoe
Sacramento River
Mono Lake
San Francisco Bay
Sierra crest
9a
1
5
6
8
1 North Coast Range
2 South Coast Range
3 Transverse Mountains
4 Peninsular Ranges
5 Cascade Range
6 Sierra Nevada
7 Tehachapi Mountains
8 Great Valley
9 Desert
a Great Basin
b Mojave
c Colorado
10 Coastal southern California

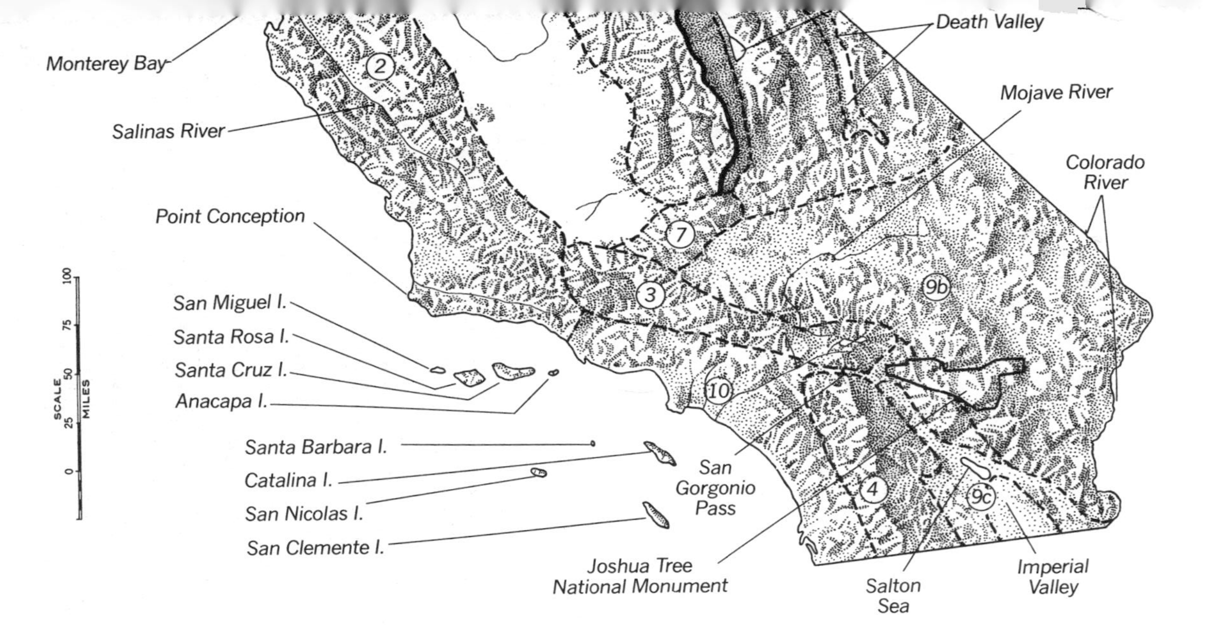

Topography and geographic areas of California. (Modified from California Insect Survey Map, Department of Entomology and Parasitology, University of California, Berkeley.)

travel in groups to breeding sites. Larvae usually of pond type (p. 17) sometimes failing to transform. Such delayed larvae are called "neotenic," and if they breed as larvae they are called "paedogenic." Confined to North America.

Tiger Salamander *(Ambystoma tigrinum)* (Pl. 1)
Identification: 3–6½ in. Black with large cream-colored or yellowish spots; two small tubercles on underside of each foot. *Habitat:* Grassland and open woodland of foothills and valleys. Breeds in reservoirs, ponds, large temporary rain pools, lakes, and slowly flowing streams. *Range:* Central Valley, including Sierran foothills and coastal region, from Napa and Yolo Counties to Kern County and vicinity of Lompoc, Santa Barbara County. Isolated population at Grass Lake, Siskyou County. Grass Lake animals are olive with cream or yellowish spots, resembling individuals from eastern Washington; perhaps introduced. Tiger Salamander larvae are commonly sold as fish bait. Near sea level to around 4,500 ft. *Habits:* Breeds January and February. Eggs (Fig. 1, p. 18) laid singly or in small clusters usually attached to vegetation in shallows. Larva (Fig. 1) often reaches 3 inches in length before metamorphosis; gill rakers on third arch, 17 or more. *Food:* Earthworms, snails, insects, fish and small mammals. Larvae eat amphipods, copepods, ostracods, midges, snails, and tadpoles.

Long-toed Salamander *(Ambystoma macrodactylum)*
Identification: 2⅛–3¼ in. Dusky or black above with metallic gold or brassy blotches (occasionally a nearly continuous stripe) on back from head to tip of tail; sides frosted with fine white flecks; tubercles on underside of feet as in Tiger Salamander. *Habitat:* Open woodland or forest, often with clearings of grass or other low-growing vegetation, to sagebrush semidesert. Breeds in lakes, ponds, and slower parts of streams. Found beneath and within rotting logs, under stones, beneath bark of logs and stumps, usually not far from water.

Range: Sierra and Cascade mountains from Tuolumne County northward; across northern part of state from Siskiyou to Warner Mountains; isolated populations in coastal Santa Cruz County. Near sea level to around 9,000 ft. *Habits:* Breeds January and February in lowlands and, after snow melts, in May, June and probably July in higher mountains. Male amplexes female in manner of newt; rubs her snout with his chin; leads female over spermatophore with tail extending upward, sometimes almost vertically. Eggs (Fig. 1) laid singly or in small groups in shallows on bottom or attached to grasses, spike rush or other objects in water. Larva (Fig. 1) of pond type but no strip of poison glands on tail and 9 to 13 gill rakers on third gill arch (Tiger Salamander has 17 or more). Overwinters at high altitude, transforming second summer. *Food:* Insects (spring-tails, flies, mosquitoes, crickets, grasshoppers, caterpillars, beetles), centipedes, pill bugs, earthworms, snails and slugs; some scavenging. Larvae eat insects (midges, water-boatmen, beetles), copepods, ostracods, snails, leeches, annelid worms, and tadpoles.

Subspecies *croceum* (Santa Cruz Long-toed Salamander) known from only two ponds in Santa Cruz County, classed as *Endangered* (p. 36).

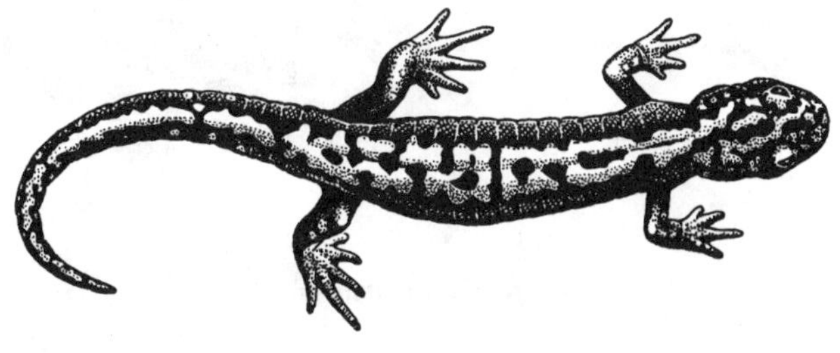

Long-toed Salamander.

Northwestern Salamander *(Ambystoma gracile)*
Well supplied with poison glands. When disturbed may assume stance resembling Ensatina (p. 7), lashing with

tail and tipping head in butting pose; whitish poison exudes from head, back, and upper surface of tail.

Identification: 3–4½ in. Brown or nearly black above; *parotoid glands* (two large swellings on back of head) and glandular thickening along upper border of tail. No foot tubercles (p. 44). Head glands and costal grooves distinguish these salamander from newts. *Habitat:* Grassland, woodland, or forest. Found under rocks, boards, and logs near ponds, lakes, and streams. *Range:* Humid coast from mouth of Gualala River, Sonoma County northward. *Habits:* Breeds January to May. In courting, male nudges and butts female and then engages in amplexes in manner of newt. Eggs in large, globular, firm-jellied clumps, about 2–5 inches in diameter, attached to roots, branches, or other firm support in quiet or slowly flowing water; algae inside egg capsules may impart greenish cast. Larva (Fig. 1) resembles Tiger Salamander but has strip of poison glands at base of dorsal fin which exudes whitish secretion when larva disturbed; larval breeding occurs; at some localities (Marion Lake, British Columbia) almost entire "adult" population is paedogenic (p. 44). *Food:* Probably insects, worms, mollusks fish, and frogs.

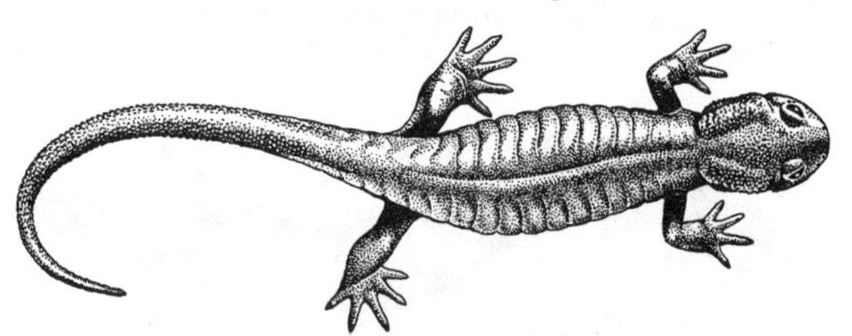

Northwestern Salamander.

Pacific Giant Salamander
(Dicamptodon ensatus) (Pl. 1)

Formidable looking because of large size and chunky head but harmless. May "growl" or "bark" when molested. Only salamander with vocal cords.

Identification: 4½–6 in. Above brown or metallic gray with marblings and spots of black or dark brown (hence often called Marbled Salamander); indistinct costal grooves (Fig. 6a); no foot tubercles (p. 44). *Habitat:* Chiefly moist forests, within and near clear, cold, rocky streams or seepages; at high altitude frequents rock-bordered lakes, where trees scarce. *Range:* Coast Range from Hecker Pass, Santa Clara County, northward; inland in mountains of northern California, around upper end of Sacramento Valley, to headwaters of Shasta Reservoir. Near sea level to over 7,000 ft. *Habits:* Breeding habits poorly known but several observations suggest following. Eggs (Fig. 1) laid in May in concealed locations several feet beneath surface in cold slowly flowing water of springs, channels under stream banks, and beneath rocks in stream bottoms; attended by female who may guard them against cannibalism of males; incubation period around 9 months; 70 to 146 eggs per clutch (based on three clutches), attached singly by short peduncles; ova whitish, unpigmented, to around ¼ inch in diameter and surrounded by thick jelly capsules. Larva (Fig. 1) of stream type; bushy dark red gills; above with dark and light mottling; light stripe behind eye; transforms at 6 to 8 inches but neotenic larvae (see p. 44) may reach nearly 1 foot in length. *Food:* Adults feed on snails, slugs, insects, shrews, mice, other amphibians, and small snakes. Larvae eat crustaceans, insects, spiders, snails, eggs of Olympic Salamander and Tailed Frog tadpoles; may scavenge.

Olympic Salamander *(Rhyacotriton olympicus)*

Identification: 1⅝–2½ in. Tail short and flat-sided; eyes large; vent lobes in male prominent and square-cut; above mottled olive and dusky; below greenish-yellow and dark-flecked. *Habitat:* Humid woods, in or near fast cold streams or seepages. When on land found under rocks or other objects usually in splash zone where ground thoroughly wet. Usually in well-shaded environments with moss and ferns. *Range:* Humid parts of north Coast Range from vicinity of Elk, Mendocino County, northward. Farthest interior localities are in westernmost Trinity County. *Habits:* Found throughout year. Eggs (Fig. 1) known only from two clusters (no adults in attendance), each of 16 eggs, found in mid-December in cracks in sandstone in spring; eggs without special organs of attachment, laid singly; presumed to have been deposited by at least three females in late October or early November; hatched in laboratory mostly during last 2 weeks in May; hatchlings averaging about an inch in total length. Larva (Fig 1) of stream type; gills reduced to nubbins; above olive, flecked with black; transforms at near adult size. *Food:* Insects (spring-tails, stoneflies, may-fly nymphs, caddis-fly larvae, beetles, flies, hymenoptera), amphipods, spiders, millipedes, snails, and worms.

Olympic Salamander.

Newts and Relatives (Family Salamandridae)

Newts differ from all other California salamanders in having rough and rather dry skin when on land. With fall and winter rains they emerge from underground retreats and rotten logs to forage. In winter and spring they enter water to breed. Males develop a smooth, swollen skin, prominent tail fins, swollen vent region, and rough dark-colored areas on undersides of feet (see illus.), which aid them in clinging to slippery body of

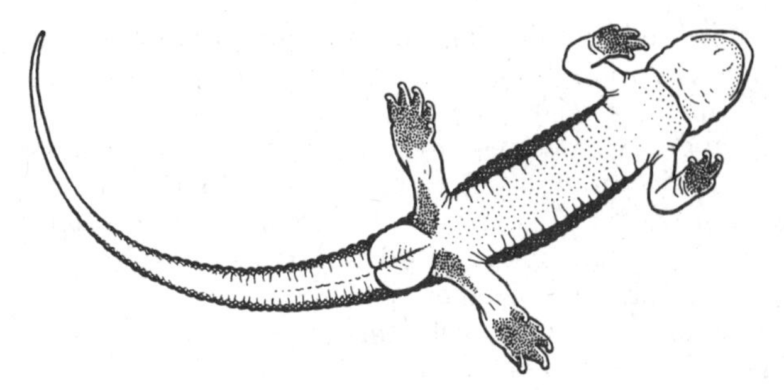

Characteristics of a breeding male newt.

female when mating. Skin change is thought to prevent males from becoming waterlogged during long periods spent in water awaiting females, and flattened tail is used as sculling organ in swimming. Females change little and leave water soon after laying their eggs.

In mating, male rides piggy-back on female and rubs her snout with his chin; skin glands there inhibit her struggles to escape. Pair separates, male deposits spermatophore, and female is lead over it as she follows male with her snout near his vent. She picks up sperm cap-

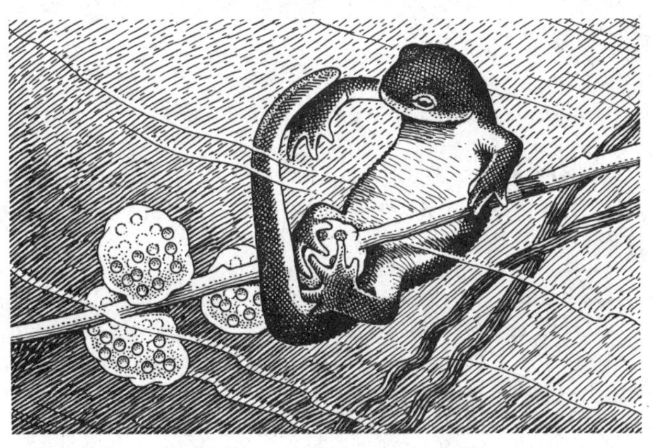

California Newt laying eggs.

sule with her vent. Eggs in firm-jellied clumps attached to sticks, roots, rocks, and other objects in water.

More active in daytime than other Californian salamanders, sometimes seen migrating to breeding sites in bright sunlight. Poisonous skin secretion protects against most predators. Defensive posture (see illus.), assumed when newt is disturbed, reveals bright orange or reddish ventral color, perhaps as warning. Tap a newt on its back to evoke this display. Dorsal surfaces plain brown or black, usually blending with surroundings.

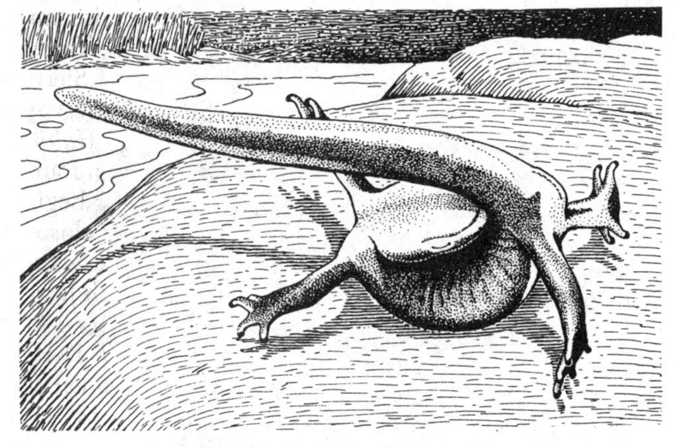

California Newt in defense pose.

Newts home to their breeding sites with great accuracy, apparently navigating by means of either sun or stars and recognizing site by odor.

California Newt *(Taricha torosa)* (Pl. 1)

Identification: 2¾–3½ in. Above tan to dark brown; below orange to pale yellow; dorsal color grades into ventral color on sides; lower eyelid and upper lip below eye usually without dark pigment (Fig. 6f); eyes large, extending to outline of head as viewed from above (Fig. 6c); teeth in roof of mouth often in Y-shaped pattern.

Occasionally grotesquely warty individuals occur at some localities in southern part of range (Boulder Creek, San Diego County). *Habitat:* Woodland, often interspersed with grassland; breeds in streams, ponds, lakes, and reservoirs; streams usually have rocky beds and bordering trees with exposed roots immersed in water, providing cover and attachment sites for eggs. In Sierra, frequents clear rocky streams, often where there is considerable current. *Range:* Coastal mountains from north-central Mendocino County south; unrecorded from humid outer coast north of San Francisco Bay; in southern California frequents drainages on south side San Gabriel and San Bernardino Mountains and western slope of Peninsular Ranges to Boulder Creek, San Diego County; throughout western slope of Sierra; isolated population in headwaters of Shasta Reservoir, Shasta County. Near sea level to around 5,000 ft. *Habits:* Mates September to May, but eggs have not been found earlier than December. Movement toward water begins in January in Sierra. Eggs (Fig. 1) in globular cluster, ¾ to 1¼ inches in diameter, usually in shallow water. Larva (p. 17) of pond type; above yellowish with longitudinal black stripe on each side at base of dorsal fin; usually under 2½ inches at transformation. *Food:* Earthworms, snails, slugs, sowbugs, insects. Larvae eat insects (including mosquito larvae), crustaceans, and scavenge.

Rough-skinned Newt *(Taricha granulosa)*

Cold-tolerant species that ranges north to southeastern Alaska. Our most aquatic newt.

Identification: 2¼–3½ in. Resembles California Newt but usually darker above and less often pale yellow below, more often orange or reddish; dorsal color stops abruptly on sides; lower eyelid and upper lip below eye usually dark-colored (Fig. 6g); eyes small, not extending to outline of head as viewed from above (Fig. 6d); teeth in roof of mouth usually in V-shaped pattern. Curls tip of tail when in defense posture (p. 50) (California Newt usually holds tail straight). *Habitat:* Similar to that of California Newt but generally cooler and more humid. *Range:* North Coast Range from Santa Cruz County northward; inland through Siskiyou Mountains into Cascades and south in Sierra to Butte County. Overlaps range of California Newt along central coast, Mendocino County south. Reported in Webber Creek, El Dorado County, along with California Newt (Sierran form), and in northeastern suburbs of Sacramento. Sea level to around 9,000 ft. *Habits:* Breeds December to July, later months to north and at high altitudes. Eggs resemble California Newt's (Fig. 1) but usually laid singly, attached to vegetation or other objects in water. Larva differs from California Newt's in lacking dark stripes (except when first hatched) and in having two rows of light spots on sides which may join to form light stripe. To 3 inches at transformation. *Food:* Snails, earthworms, crustaceans, spiders, insects, amphibian eggs, freshwater sponges, and some plant material; scavenges.

Red-bellied Newt (*Taricha rivularis*) (Pl. 1)

The name *rivularis* (river-dwelling) refers to its stream-dwelling habits.

Identification: 2¾–3¼ in. Readily distinguished from other Californian newts by its dark eyes and tomato-red ventral color with broad dark stripe across vent; dorsal color stops abruptly on sides; lower eyelid and upper lid below eye light-colored. *Habitat:* Woodland or forest streams. *Range:* Coast Range from Russian River and vicinity of Agua Caliente, Sonoma County and Lower Lake, Lake County to Honeydew, Humboldt County. Coexists with Rough-skinned Newt but usually in faster water. *Habits:* Breeds March to May. Eggs resemble California Newt's but in "streamlined" flattened clusters, usually attached to undersides of stones or branches in flowing water; clusters sometimes in large aggregations. Larva plain colored above; dorsal fin does not extend beyond forelimbs.

Lungless Salamanders (Family Plethodontidae)

Largest group of salamanders; all in New World except 2 species of web-toes (p. 65) in Europe. All are lungless and breathe through their thin moist skin; a few have permanent gills; all have hair-line furrow (nasolabial groove) from each nostril to edge of lip (examine with magnifying glass). Grooves transport water by capillary action to nose and Jacobson's Organs, special sensory areas in the nose, as salamander taps snout against moist ground. This behavior is thought to aid these salamanders in tracking one another or in recognizing familiar terrain. Most Californian lungless salamanders are strictly nocturnal and land-dwelling, but several species occasionally briefly enter water.

Jelly-coated eggs with large, cream-colored unpigmented ova, ⅛ to ¼ inch in diameter (Fig. 1) laid on land —underground, beneath objects, or in rotten wood and, in most (all Californian species), development is direct,

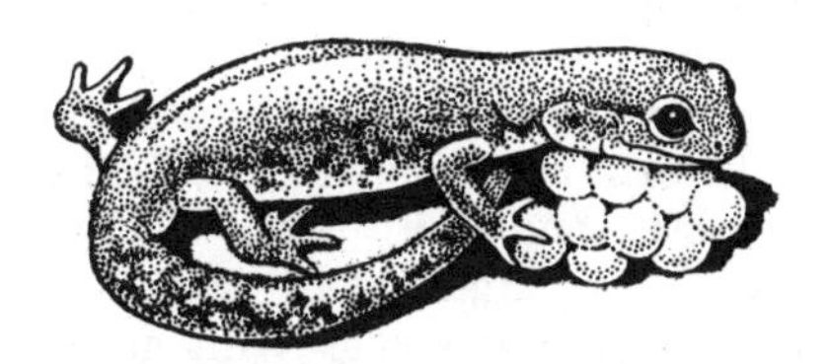

Female Ensatina brooding her eggs.

without larval stages; some species brood their eggs. Large gills of embryo lost at time of hatching. Young hatch in summer or fall (slender slamanders excepted) resembling adults in all but a few species in eastern United States.

Woodland Salamanders *(Plethodon)*

This is the largest group of lungless salamanders in the United States but there are only 3 species in California. Slender, rather short-legged, with prominent costal grooves (Fig. 6a); often with broad longtitudinal stripe from head to tip of tail. Ground-dwelling. Large-yolked, unpigmented eggs usually laid in clusters in rotten logs or underground.

Del Norte Salamander *(Plethodon elongatus)*

Identification: 2–3 in. Above dark brown or black often with tan dorsal stripe; stripe vague or absent in humid coastal areas; in Klamath Basin generally light brown flecked with white and longer limbed; 5 to 8 costal folds between tips of toes when limbs straightened along sides (Fig. 6b); costal grooves 18, occasionally 17 or 19 (Fig. 6a); Young more often striped than adults. *Habitat:* Chiefly rock rubble of stable talus, old riverbeds, road fills, and outcrops; occasionally under logs and other objects; soil damp but rarely soaking wet. Frequents humid coastal forests but ranges inland into mixed coniferous and broadleaf woodland. *Range:* From vicinity of Blue Lake, Humboldt County, northward; inland to vicinity of Happy Camp along Klamath River, Siskiyou County, and to Salyer along Trinity River, Trinity County. Distribution follows river drainages. To 2,500 ft. *Habits:* Active on surface from fall to spring, except during cold or dry weather. Only one egg cluster known; found July 27 attached to underside of redwood post along Smith River; 10 eggs suspended in grapelike cluster, attached by pedicels 3–4 mm. in length to common base; eggs with advanced larvae about 1 inch long; ⅜ inch in diameter to outer surface of jelly capsules; adult present. *Food:* Insects (beetles, spring-tails, caterpillars, flies, leafhoppers), millipedes, isopods, ticks, and spiders.

Del Norte Salamander.

Siskiyou Mountain Salamander
(Plethodon stormi) Rare species

Identification: 2–3 in. Similar to Del Norte Salamander but lighter brown and profusely speckled above with whitish; legs longer, only 2 to 7 costal folds between tips of toes when legs straightened along sides (Del Norte Salamander has 5 to 8 folds) (Fig. 6b); costal grooves 17, occasionally 18. Young rarely striped. *Habitat:* Old talus slopes in or near moist woods. *Range:* In California known only from two localities in northern Siskiyou County.

Dunn's Salamander *(Plethodon dunni)*

Identification: 2–3 in. Broad dorsal stripe of tan to greenish yellow, flecked with dusky, sometimes heavily so, brightening on tail; below slaty with small spots of yellowish; costal grooves 15 or 16 (Fig. 6a). *Habitat:* Similar to that of Del Norte Salamander but wetter. Rocks frequently moss-covered. Found under rocks of seepages and on stream banks, under logs and other objects. Occasionally enters water to escape. *Range:* Known only from three localities—along Smith River, Rowdy Creek, and Mill Creek, Del Norte County. *Habits:* Ova cream-colored, unpigmented, around 3/16 inches in diameter, in eggs laid in captivity.

Dunn's Salamander.

Ensatina *(Ensatina eschscholtzi)* (Pl. 2)

Tap salamander on back to evoke characteristic defense posture (p. 7). Tail may exude sticky, milky poison and is cast off at constricted base if injured, wriggling actively for several minutes.

Identification: 1½–3 in. Tail constricted at base; skin smooth. Seven distinctive subspecies: Painted Salamander—above mottled with dusky, yellow and orange; sometimes predominately one color (outer coast from northern Humboldt County north). Oregon Salamander —Plain brown or black above; leg bases yellow or orange; belly pale with fine black specks; young resemble Painted Salamander (Sonoma and Lake County, northward). Yellow-eyed Salamander—Large yellow eye patch; belly orange (coastal region from Alameda to Napa County, east and north of San Francisco Bay; foothills of Sierra, Calaveras to Madera Counties, mostly below 6,000 ft.). Hybridizes with Sierra Nevada Salamander. Monterey Salamander—Plain reddish or orange brown above; whitish below, no fine black flecks (Coastal Mountains, Paso Robles, San Luis Obispo County south to San Diego County; crest and south slope of San Gabriel and San Bernardino Mountains). Sierra Nevada Salamander—Dusky or brown above with orange spots (Sierra Nevada). Yellow-blotched Salamander—Black with greenish yellow to cream spots (Tehachapi Mountains, Fort Tejon, Mount Pinos). Large-blotched Salamander—Black with large orange blotches (mountains of southern California south of San Gorgonio Pass). Hybridizes with Monterey Salamander in Mill Canyon (not Mill Creek Canyon) north of Banning and on Mount Palomar. Areas between subspecies occupied by populations with intermediate characteristics. *Habitat:* Damp woodland and forest, often in vicinity of streams. Rotting logs and leaf litter usually abundant. Found in rotten logs, under bark, beneath logs and rocks and in woodrat nests. Near sea level to above 10,000 feet (in rocky habitat) on Mount San Gorgonio. *Range:* Throughout California except floor of Great Valley, desert, and dry regions of Cascade–Sierran crest. Distribution spotty.

Large blotched and Monterey Salamanders are terminal forms of plain-colored and spotted subspecies that are connected in mountains of northern California. Spotted forms occur in Sierra Nevada and higher mountains of southern California and plain-colored forms in Coast Ranges. The two subspecies lines are separated by the Great Valley but come together to south where the two mountain systems meet (see map). Spotted subspecies generally occur at higher elevation than plain-colored

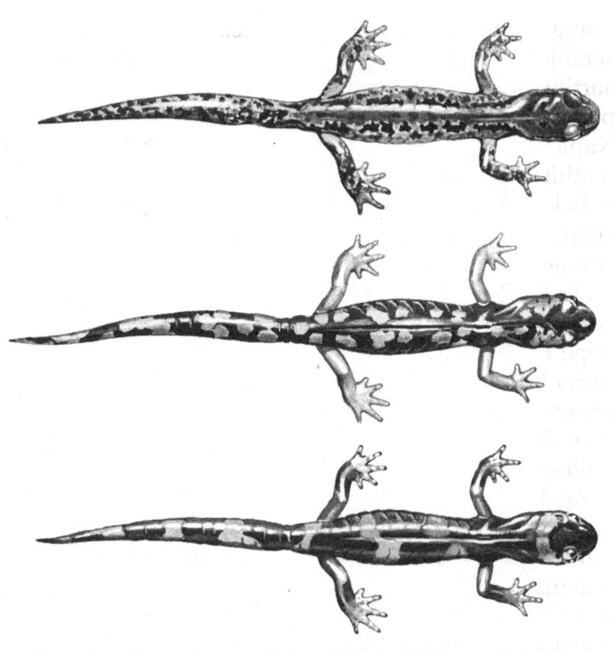

Ensatina. From above to below—Painted Salamander, Sierra Nevada Salamander, and Large-blotched Salamander.

ones, frequenting coniferous forests or mixed broadleaf and coniferous woodland. Plain-colored subspecies occur primarily in broad-leaf woodland and streamside growth. *Habits:* Active October or November to May. Mates from October to end of March. Male noses female and rubs her throat with his body (p. 16,a). She places her chin against upper surface of base of his tail and he leads her about, sometimes for several hours (b). As she picks up spermatophore, he strokes her back with his tail (c). Eggs laid in late spring or early summer in underground locations or beneath bark or inside rotten logs. Ova unpigmented, to about ¼ inch in diameter; eggs in loose grapelike cluster (Fig. 1). Female protects them from drying and other animals. Brooding stops at hatching, and young must fend for themselves. Hatchlings, along with adults, appear on surface with first rains. *Food:* Earthworms, sow bugs, millipedes, centipedes, spiders, insects, (including termites, camel crickets, and beetles).

Slender Salamanders *(Batrachoseps)*

Slim bodied, usually with long tail, very small limbs, and four toes on both front and hind feet (other Californian salamanders have five toes on hind feet); conspicuous costal and caudal grooves, (Fig. 6a), giving segmented, wormlike appearance, hence called "Worm Salamanders"; in males upper jaw teeth perforate lip. Small size and reduced limbs permit most species to enter termite and earthworm burrows, and other small openings.

Eight species, seven in California, differing in size, proportions (limb and tail length, foot size, head width), and coloration; not easily distinguished; use locality of occurrence as a help in making identifications.

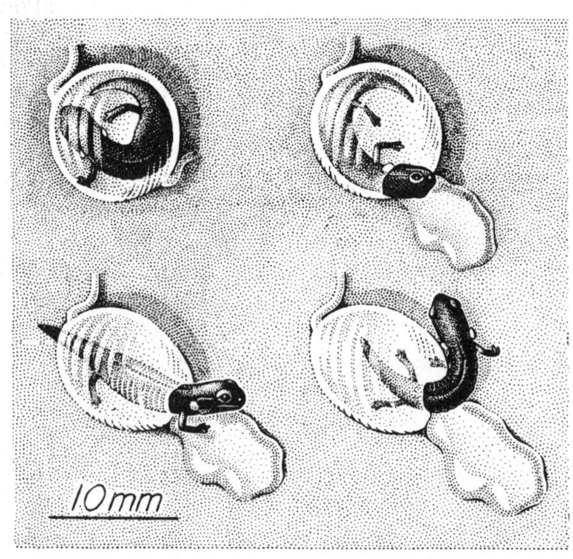

Hatching of a slender salamander.

Eggs laid in moist places on land, in hollows under ground and occasionally beneath logs and rocks. California and Garden Slender Salamanders lay during winter rainy season and differ in this respect from all other western salamanders. Females with large yellowish eggs evident through abdominal wall, found after first rains in fall or winter. Eggs of Relictual Slender Salamander found in large numbers in May at Sugar Pine, Madera County, 4,300 feet, beneath objects on banks of a shallow stream. Eggs jelly-coated, ova pigmented, to almost 3/16 inch in diameter; capsules more or less connected by jelly strands (Fig. 1).

Found in damp places under boards, logs, rocks, and other surface objects, inside and beneath bark of logs and in moist rock slides. Relictual Salamander unusual in some areas in occurring under objects in wet surroundings, often in film of water at edges of springs and seepages.

When first exposed, may be found in a coil like a watch spring, and if handled roughly may flip about violently or wriggle away rapidly in snakelike fashion. If tail seized, it may snap off and thrash about while salamander crawls beneath nearby object and "freezes." Thrashing tail may divert attention of predators; a new tail is grown.

Found from October to May depending on soil moisture conditions and temperature; Relictual Slender Salamander all year in springs and seepages.

Food: Earthworms, small slugs, snails, sowbugs, millipedes, mites, spiders, and insects (spring-tails, thrips, aphids, caterpillars, flies, small beetles, and ants).

California Slender Salamander
(Batrachoseps attenuatus)

1–2 in. Ten to 12 costal folds between tips of toes when limbs straightened along sides (Fig. 6b); head small, limbs short; ventral color dark gray to black, under magnification seen as dense network of melanophores; guanophores (fine white flecks) abundant on nearly all ventral surfaces; dorsal color highly variable; broad dorsal stripe of reddish, beige, brown, or dusky, continuous or broken into patches, sometimes absent; sides of body and most of dorsal surface of limbs and head brown or blackish. *Range:* Coast Ranges from southwestern Oregon to Santa Ana Mountains; southern slope Transverse Mountains; western foothills of Sierra Nevada. A foothill and mountain form ranging into pine zone in southern California.

Garden Slender Salamander *(Batrachoseps major)* Head broader and limbs relatively longer than in California Slender Salamander; ventral color whitish, light gray or yellowish with melanophores broken into spots or partial network (not a dense net), guanophores sparse or absent from middle of belly and ventrally on tail; dorsal color pink to purplish with or without broad central stripe of brick red, usually composed of dashes and streaks; sides of body and dorsal surfaces of limbs and head light colored. *Range:* Mostly coastal southern California from base of Transverse Mountains south into Baja California; Catalina Island. Coexists with California Slender Salamander at number of localities in Los Angeles basin and in Santa Ana Mountains (Irvine Park). Frequents chiefly alluvial deposits of lowlands, gardens, and generally occurs at lower elevations than California Slender Salamander.

Garden Slender Salamander.

Pacific Slender Salamander *(Batrachoseps pacificus)* Coloration resembles that of Garden Slender Salamander but head broader, hind limbs longer, feet larger, and tail shorter. *Range:* Santa Barbara Islands—Anacapa, Santa Cruz, Santa Rosa, and San Miguel.

Kern Canyon Slender Salamander
(Batrachoseps simatus) Rare species
Coloration resembles that of California Slender Salamander but body more robust, head broader, limbs longer, and feet larger; 6 to 9½ costal folds between tips of toes when limbs straightened along sides (Fig. 6b); costal grooves 19–20 (Fig. 6a); gunanophores abundant midventrally on belly and tail. *Range:* Kern River Canyon, Kern County. Coexists with Relictual Slender Salamander at Cow Flat and Stork Creeks. Salamanders at Fairview, 3,500 ft., Tulare County, tentatively included in this species.

Tehachapi Slender Salamander
(Batrachoseps stebbinsi) Rare species
Similar to Kern Canyon Slender Salamander but larger, more robust, with broader head and longest limbs of any of our species; toes webbed, only terminal joint free (1½ to 2 joints free in Kern Canyon form). *Range:* Piute and Tehachapi Mountains, Kern County.

Relictual Slender Salamander *(Batrachoseps relictus)*
Coloration similar to California Slender Salamander but body more robust, limbs longer, head wider; small species, adults rarely over 2 inches in snout-vent length; differs from Kern Canyon and Tehachapi forms in small size and generally having fewer costal grooves (16 to 20 vs. 19 to 20) (Fig. 6a), shorter legs, and vomerine teeth arranged in single row rather than in patches. *Range:* Sierra Nevada from Merced River, Mariposa County, to Kern River Canyon, Kern County, 600 to 8,100 feet; Coast Range in western Monterey and northern San Luis Obispo Counties, sea level to 4,000 feet; Santa Cruz Island, Santa Barbara County; San Pedro Martir Mountains, around 7,000 feet, Baja California. Coexists with California Slender Salamander at a num-

ber of localities in Sierra and Coast Range, with Kern River Salamander in Kern River Canyon, and with Pacific Slender Salamander on Santa Cruz Island.

Desert Slender Salamander
(Batrachoseps aridus) Endangered species

1¼–2 in. Head and limbs longer and feet proportionally larger than in other species; black to chocolate-maroon above with indistinct broad dorsal stripe composed of silver to brassy flecks; tail flesh-colored below, contrasting with remaining dark ventral color. *Habitat and Range:* Known only from Hidden Palm Canyon, desert slope of mountains south of Palm Desert, around 2,500 ft., Riverside County. Vegetation of cholla, agave, barrel cactus, prickly pear, creosote bush, manzanita, juniper, and mesquite on exposed slopes and sugar bush, willow, and Washington Palms on canyon floor. Found under rocks and within crevices of limestone seepages.

Climbing Salamanders *(Aneides)*

Strong-jawed lungless salamanders with prominent jaw muscles, which often give head triangular shape from above, especially in males; upper jaw teeth project below lip (Fig. 6e) and can usually be felt if snout stroked; conspicuous costal and caudal grooves (Fig. 6a); toes usually with squarish tips.

Three species in California. Arboreal and Clouded Salamanders are excellent climbers but Black Salamander is chiefly ground-dwelling.

Jelly-coated eggs in clusters, suspended by intertwined strands of jelly usually united at common base; ova cream-colored, unpigmented 3/16 to 1/4 in. diam. (Fig. 1); laid in cavities in rotting logs, trees or underground, and brooded; develop in summer.

Arboreal Salamander *(Aneides lugubris)* (Pl. 2)
Identification: 2½–3¾ in. Brown above with pale yellow spots; spots vary greatly in size and number, de-

Arboreal Salamanders guarding eggs.

pending upon locality, and may be scarce or absent (in Sierra); toes with squarish tips; costal grooves 15, occasionally 14 or 16 (Fig. 6a); tail somewhat prehensile. Young clouded with fine gray speckling and with brassy patch on snout, on each shoulder, at each limb base and on tail. *Habitat:* Chiefly oak woodland but ranges into mixed pines and oaks in Sierra. Found in tree hollows, under bark, inside rotting logs, and beneath logs, bark, rocks, and other objects on ground; often found in crevices in walls. *Range:* Coast Ranges from northern Humboldt County to Baja California; Sierran foothills from El Dorado to Madera Counties; South Farallon, Año Nuevo, and Catalina Islands. To around 4,000 ft. in Sierra. *Habits:* Arboreal and terrestrial. May gather in large numbers in moist hollows, sometimes high above ground, in coast and interior live oaks and other trees during dry summer weather. Active on surface October or November to May, except during cold or dry spells. Eggs (Fig. 1) may be deposited in arboreal or terrestrial sites. *Food:* Insects (beetles, caterpillars, ants), centipedes, spiders, sowbugs, slender salamanders, and probably fungus.

Clouded Salamander *(Aneides ferreus)*

Identification: 2–3 in. Slimmer, and with less triangular head than Arboreal Salamander: 16 or 17 costal grooves (Fig. 6a); above mottled black or dark brown and pale gray to whitish with flecks of brassy ("clouded" coloration). Young resembles that of Arboreal Salamander but slimmer. *Habitat:* Humid coastal forest, especially within and at edges of clearings. Usually found under loosening dead bark of Douglas fir logs with firm heartwood; also occurs beneath leaf litter on top of fissured sawed stumps and under loose bark of stumps; occasionally beneath objects on ground. *Range:* From northern Sonoma County north throughout Coast Range. *Habits:* Most agile climber among Californian salamanders. Eggs found beneath bark and in hollows in rotten logs in summer. *Food:* Insects (ants, beetles, spring-tails, termites, and fly larvae), spiders, centipedes, and millipedes.

Clouded Salamander.

Black Salamander *(Aneides flavipunctatus)* (Pl. 2)

Identification: 2⅝–3 in. Differs from other climbing salamanders in having shorter legs, 3 to 5 costal folds between tips of toes when limbs straightened along sides (1 to 1½ folds in others) (Fig. 6b); toes shorter and with rounded tips. Coloration highly variable, depending upon locality: Black above, sometimes with small white flecks (south of Golden Gate); large spots, cream-colored (Sonoma and Mendocino Counties) or white (Napa, Lake, and Glenn Counties) on black ground color; spotting reduced or absent and dorsal surfaces suffused with fine gray flecks, greenish in light phase (northern Mendocino County, northward, especially in

Plate 1. a, *California Newt, land stage (*b, *male in aquatic stage);* c, *Red-bellied Newt;* d, *Pacific Giant Salamander;* e, *Tiger Salamander.*

Plate 2. a, *Ensatina (Yellow-eyed Salamander);* b, *Arboreal Salamander* (d, *young);* e, *Black Salamander from south of Golden Gate* (c, *young;* f, *adult from north of San Francisco Bay);* g, *California Slender Salamander, red type* (h, *brown type).*

Plate 3. a, *Western Spadefoot Toad;* b, *Western Toad;* c, *Yellow-legged Frog* (d, *ventral surface);* e, *Red-legged Frog* (f, *ventral surface);* g, *Bullfrog;* h, *Pacific Treefrog, brown type* (i, *green type).*

Plate 4. a, *Western Whiptail;* b, *Sagebrush Lizard* (d, *ventral surface);* c, *Western Fence Lizard* (e, *ventral surface);* f, *Coast Horned Lizard.*

Plate 5. a, *Side-blotched Lizard;* b, *young Gilbert's Skink* (c, *adult);* d, *young Western Skink* (e, *adult);* f, *California Legless Lizard.*

Plate 6. a, *Southern Alligator Lizard;* b, *Northern Alligator Lizard;* c, *Sharp-tailed Snake;* d, *Western Black-headed Snake;* e, *Night Snake;* f, *Long-nosed Snake;* g, *Glossy Snake;* h, *Coachwhip.*

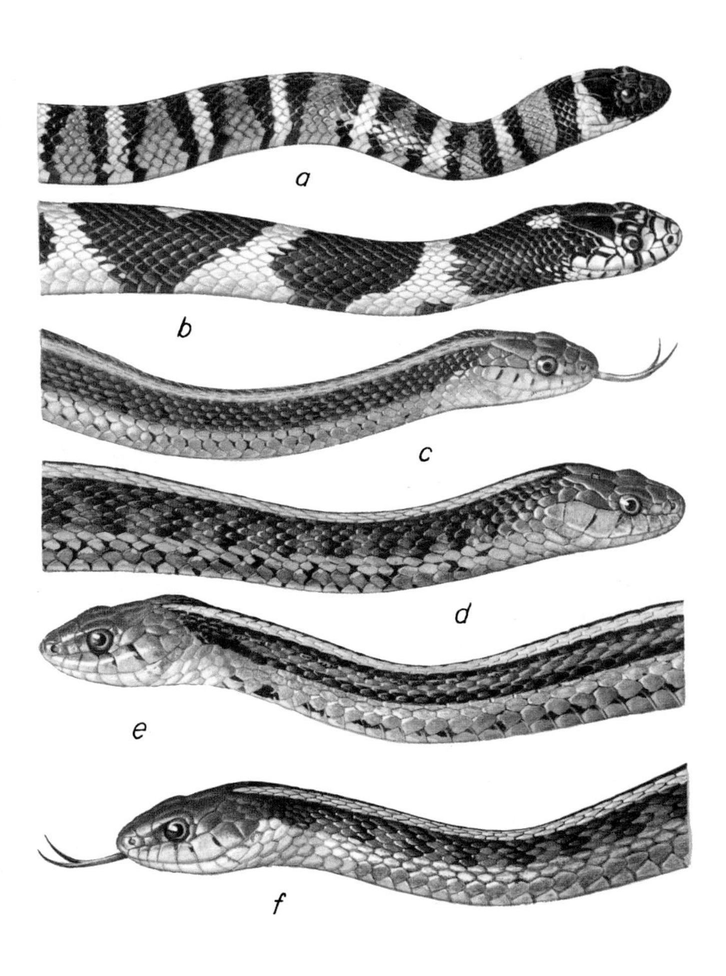

Plate 7. a, *California Mountain Kingsnake;* b, *Common Kingsnake;* c, *Western Aquatic Garter Snake;* d, *Western Terrestrial Garter Snake;* f, *Common Garter Snake* (e, *from San Francisco Peninsula*).

Plate 8. a, *Gopher Snake;* b, *Western Rattlesnake;* c, *young Racer* (d, *adult*); e, *Striped Racer;* f, *Western Ringneck Snake;* g, *Rubber Boa.*

redwood areas); black with many small white flecks (Trinity and Shasta Counties); all varieties have dark ventral ground color. Young generally dark with varying amounts of brassy flecking and yellow limb bases; in northern Mendocino County northward, young in light phase often vivid emerald green and limb bases bright lemon yellow. *Habitat:* Chiefly mixed coniferous and broadleaf forest in vicinity of streams or seepages. In cooler areas found at edges of or within clearings. Occurs under rocks and logs, beneath bark and inside rotting logs, in leaf- or moss-covered talus, rocky seepages, and under rocks in wet places at edges of streams. Populations south of Golden Gate often in thoroughly wet places but those in Lake and Glenn Counties in less wet surroundings. *Range:* Coast Range from Santa Cruz and Santa Clara Counties north; in northern part of range inland to Shasta Reservoir, Shasta County. *Habits:* Active on surface from beginning of fall or winter rains to May except during cold or dry weather; in wet surroundings immatures may be found later in year. Eggs (Fig. 1) in cavities in ground; brooded. *Food:* Insects (beetles, etc.), spiders.

Web-toed Salamanders *(Hydromantes)*

Small group of closely related lungless salamanders yet widely separated—3 species in California and 2 in Europe. Head and body somewhat flattened; toes partly webbed; tail short, blunt-tipped, in California species used canelike as an aid in locomotion. Tail curled forward and tip placed against ground as hind foot lifted. Tongue mushroom-like, capable of protrusion to over one third body length to seize prey on sticky tip. These are climbing, crevice or cave-dwelling salamanders notable for their background-matching coloration. Males have projecting upper jaw teeth perhaps used to stimulate female when mating.

Mount Lyell Salamander *(Hydromantes platycephalus)*
Identification: 1¾–2¾ in. Granite-like coloration; flat-

test of all web-toed species; adults with ½ to 1½ costal folds between tips of toes (Fig. 6b) when limbs straightened along sides (toes overlap in others). Young greenish. *Habitat:* Granite exposures of Sierra Nevada in vicinity of seepages from streams or melting snow banks and areas wet by spray from streams or waterfalls. Much of habitat occurs where tree growth is scant; found in rocky places bordering mountain meadows. *Range:* Sierra from Sonora Pass to Twin Lakes, Silliman Gap, Sequoia National Park, 4,000 to 11,000 ft. *Habits:* Found beneath objects on surface, mostly in July and August at high elevations; April to June at lower elevations. Eggs unknown. *Food:* Centipedes, spiders, termites, beetles, and adult and larval flies.

Limestone Salamander

(Hydromantes brunus) Rare species

Identification: 2–2¾ in. Plain brown above, resembling soil color of habitat; can be confused with Arboreal Salamander which occurs in same area but Limestone Salamander has webbed toes; long-legged, tips of toes of adults overlapping about 1½ costal folds when limbs placed along sides (Fig. 6b). Young pale yellowish-green or yellowish, without pattern. *Habitat:* Limestone areas in Digger pine, canyon oak, chaparral zone in vicinity of streams or seepages. Frequents rock crevices, talus, mine shafts, and caves; under rocks and logs on surface in wet weather. *Range:* Merced Canyon and tributaries in vicinity of Briceburg and Bear Valley, Mariposa County. To 2,500 ft.

Limestone Salamander.

Shasta Salamander

(Hydromantes shastae) Rare species

Identification: 1¾–2½ in. Above less mottled than Mount Lyell Salamander, grayish green, beige or tan with yellow on tail; limbs longer, when straightened along sides of body, tips of toes overlap ½ to 1½ costal folds (Fig. 6b). *Habitat:* Limestone caves and fissures, in open forests of fir, pine, and oak. In wet weather under objects in vicinity of limestone outcrops. *Range:* Limestone areas in headwaters of Shasta Reservoir. To 2,500 ft. *Habits:* Active on surface (except during cold weather) following fall rains until onset of dry weather (May, June). Eggs in grapelike cluster, in caves in summer, attended by female; ova cream-colored, about 3/16 inch in diameter; jelly strands interwoven among jelly capsules.

FROGS AND TOADS

Ascaphids (Family Ascaphidae)

Tailed Frog *(Ascaphus truei)*

Considered member of ancient group; closest relatives are 3 species of frogs in New Zealand.

Identification: 1–2 in. Toadlike; skin rather rough; pupils vertical, fifth toe broadest; above brown, olive, or gray with pale triangle on snout. Male with short taillike copulatory organ, vent opening at tip; unique structure among frogs. *Habitat:* Humid woods with rocky cold streams and stretches of fast water. *Range:* Coast Range from vicinity of Elk, Mendocino County, northward; inland in northern part of State to McCloud River basin, Shasta County. *Habits:* Chiefly nocturnal. Breeds in fall; amplexus pelvic. Eggs (Fig. 2) laid in summer in globular masses, under stones in cold streams; ova unpigmented, to 3/16 inch in diameter, surrounded by jelly capsule and connected by jelly strands like string of beads; hatch in late summer and fall. Tadpoles (Fig. 2) dark-colored, streamlined, with large round mouth covering ⅓ ventral surface of body; tail usually with conspicuous light spot at tip; transforms 2 to 3 years after hatching. Apparently voiceless. ***Food:*** Adults eat insects (spring-tails, stonefly nymphs, beetles, flies, mayflies, and caterpillars), spiders, millipedes, amphipods, and snails. Larvae feed on diatoms and pollen (in season).

Tailed Frog (male).

Spadefoot Toads (Family Pelobatidae)

Widely distributed and of variable form and habits but species in New World, including California forms, squat, short-legged, toadlike, with vertical pupils and single black sharp-edge "spade" on hindfoot (Fig. 6). Many species, including all California forms, are adapted to live in arid or semiarid environments.

Our species breed in temporary pools after heavy rains or in slow streams, reservoirs, or irrigation ditches. Dry periods spent underground in self-made burrows or in those constructed by other animals; dig backwards into soil using foot spades.

Eggs jelly-coated (Fig. 5) in cylindrical, grapelike clusters attached to plant stems or other objects in shallow quiet water. Tadpoles (Fig. 2) ¾ inch (Couch's Spadefoot) to nearly 3 inches in total length (Western Spadefoot) at transformation; snout short, body broadest just behind eyes, which are close together well up on head; oral papillae nearly completely encircle mouth (Fig. 3). Transformation within two months or less following egg laying, in keeping with rapid drying of breeding sites.

Males have loud voice, which attracts other individuals from afar; throat dusky except in Couch's Spadefoot; amplexus pelvic.

Western Spadefoot *(Scaphiopus hammondi)* (Pl. 3)

Identification: 1½–2½ in. Above generally olive or gray, often with hourglass-like markings on back, pupils may be large and round when animal first caught but become vertical in light; "spade" on hindfoot about as wide as long (Fig. 6j). *Habitat:* Open treeless grassland or mixed woodland and grassland where temporary pools form or there are sandy, gravelly washes or small streams; streams are often temporary. *Range:* Great Valley and surrounding foothills; South Coast Range into Baja California; absent from outer cool coast north of Point Conception; formerly widespread on Los Angeles coastal plain. To around 4,500 ft. in Sierran foothills. *Habits:* Chiefly nocturnal. Constructs burrows in loose soil to depth of at least 3 feet, where it avoids temperature extremes and dryness. May congregate at favorable burrowing sites, often well removed from breeding locality. Loose soil of burrow surrounds toad. In Arizona known to spend 9 months underground, emerging with summer rains. Also uses burrows of kangaroo rats and other animals. Eggs laid in late winter and spring, transformation occurring in late spring and summer. Tadpoles olive or gray above. Adults emerge with soaking rains in fall. *Voice:* May carry ½ mile; catlike purr but stronger and hoarser; snorelike "kwalk," lasting ½ to 1¼ seconds. *Food:* Insects, worms, and other invertebrates.

Great Basin Spadefoot *(Scaphiopus intermontanus)*

Identification: 1½–2 in. Closely resembles Western Spadefoot; no satisfactory distinguishing characteristics other than voice, which cannot be adequately described; must rely on locality of occurrence (see Range, below). *Habitat:* Sagebrush flats, pinyon-juniper woodland, and mountain meadows with scattered conifers. Breeds in springs, slowly flowing streams, temporary pools, and canals. *Range:* East of Cascade–Sierran crest from northern Inyo County northward. To around 8,000 ft. *Habits:* Less strictly nocturnal than Western Spadefoot. Active May to October, especially following rains, but does not depend on rainfall for activity. Voice hoarse "walk–walk–walk," each call lasting 1/5 to 1 second; chorus suggests man sawing wood. *Food:* Insects (ants, beetles, grasshoppers, crickets), etc.

Couch's Spadefoot *(Scaphiopus couchi)*

Identification: 2¼–3½ in. Above with spots and coarse network of dusky on yellowish ground color; eyes separated by width of upper eyelid or more (less than eyelid width in other Spadefoots); spade sickle-shaped. *Habitat:* Arid and semiarid regions—short grass plains, mesquite savannah, and brushy desert. California populations occur along washes in creosote bush desert. *Range:* Known only from extreme southeastern part of state at Glamis, Imperial County, and 15 miles north of Vidal Junction, San Bernardino County. *Habits:* Nocturnal. In California Glamis population becomes active after thundershowers when water flows in washes. Aridity is so great breeding may not occur every year. Eggs resemble Western Spadefoot's but smaller (Fig. 2). Tadpoles in Arizona with coppery bronze ground color (California tadpoles undescribed). Voice distinctive, plaintive bleat or "meow," lasting ¾ to 1¼ seconds.

True Toads (Family Bufonidae)

Worldwide. Stocky, short-legged, broad-waisted, warty, toothless, anurans with pair of large glands (parotoids) on back of head; pair of well-developed tubercles on hind feet; ridges, cranial crests, usually frame upper eyelids on top head. Warts and parotoids contain poison glands which secrete sticky, milky fluid that repels some predators and irritates human eyes. Toads do not cause warts.

Habitats of California forms vary from desert to high mountain meadows, from hot dry areas to snow melt pools at timberline. Chiefly terrestrial but enter water to breed. Often progress by walking as well as by hopping.

Many capable of burrowing in loose soil to considerable depths by means of tubercles on hind feet. Most of our species lay eggs in gelatinous strings (Fig. 2). Tadpoles are often dark-colored; eyes well in from outline of head as viewed from above; fringe of oral papillae confined to sides of mouth and indented (Fig. 3). Amplexus pectoral.

Colorado River Toad *(Bufo alvarius)*

Identification: 3–6 in. Our largest toad; dark brown or olive above, with smooth skin, long kidney-shaped parotoids, and prominent cranial crests; several large warts on hind legs stand out conspicuously against smooth skin; a whitish knob at angle of mouth. *Habitat:* Brushy desert with creosote bush and mesquite; farmland. Frequents washes, springs, river bottoms, temporary rain pools, canals, and irrigation ditches. *Range:* Lower Colorado River and irrigated lowlands of Imperial County. *Habits:* Nocturnal. More aquatic than most toads. Seeks refuge in burrows of other animals. Most active from May to July. Eggs, to around 8,000, in long strings; jelly envelope single. Voice resembles ferryboat whistle but weak, hoots lasting ½ to 1 second. Throat pale in male; vocal sac weak. When molested assumes butting pose and may squirt poison over 10 ft. from parotoid glands; poison, if swallowed in quantity, capable of paralyzing and occasionally killing dogs. Coons disembowel these toads and eat internal organs only. *Food:* Insects (grasshoppers, bugs, beetles, termites, ants, wasps, moths, and caterpillars), spiders, scorpions, centipedes, snails, small lizards, other amphi-

Colorado River Toad.

bians (toads, spadefoots), and mice. Comes to outdoor lights to catch insects.

Great Plains Toad *(Bufo cognatus)*

Identification: 2–4½ in. Large well-defined dark blotches in pairs on back; cranial crests diverge widely posteriorly and are more or less united on snout to form boss; parotoids oval; sometimes narrow dorsal stripe down middle of back. *Habitat:* Grassland and deserts; truly a plains toad. *Range:* Colorado River bottom lands and irrigated lowlands of Imperial County north to vicinity of Indio, Riverside County, where it occurs in date palm orchards. Apparently has dispersed northward along irrigation canals. *Habits:* Chiefly nocturnal. Breeds April to September in shallow temporary pools or quiet water of streams, irrigation ditches, or flooded fields. Eggs in slender scalloped strings, to as many as 20,000 per female. Voice a harsh, explosive, metallic clatter, resembling pneumatic hammer, lasting 5 to 20 seconds; at close range chorus almost deafening; inflated vocal sac sausage-shaped, ⅓ size of body. *Food:* Moths, caterpillars, flies, beetles, and other insects.

Great Plains Toad.

Red-spotted Toad *(Bufo punctatus)*

Identification: 1½–3 in. Head and body flattened, an adaptation for crevice-dwelling; parotoids small and round; snout pointed; cranial crests weak; often has granite-matching pattern and reddish-tipped warts. Male with dusky throat. Young have orange-tipped warts and undersides of feet are yellow. *Habitat:* Desert, open grassland, brushland, palm oases, oak woods. Frequents springs, seepages, intermittent stream courses, and cattle tanks. *Range:* Throughout desert from northern Inyo County south into Mexico, hence often called "Desert Toad." Natural hybrids with Woodhouse's Toad known from Colorado. *Habits:* Chiefly nocturnal but often diurnal when breeding. Breeds when opportunity affords, April (Death Valley) to September. Eggs with one jelly envelope, laid singly in short strings or loose flat clusters on bottom of small, shallow, often rocky, pools. Tadpoles resemble those of

Western Toad (Fig. 2) but have coarser spotting on dorsal fin, and upper labium and tooth rows extend downward on each side of mouth. Voice a clear bird-like trill lasting 4 to 10 seconds, on one pitch but occasionally dropping toward end; often heard just after sunset; vocal sac round. *Food:* Beetles, ants, bees, and other insects.

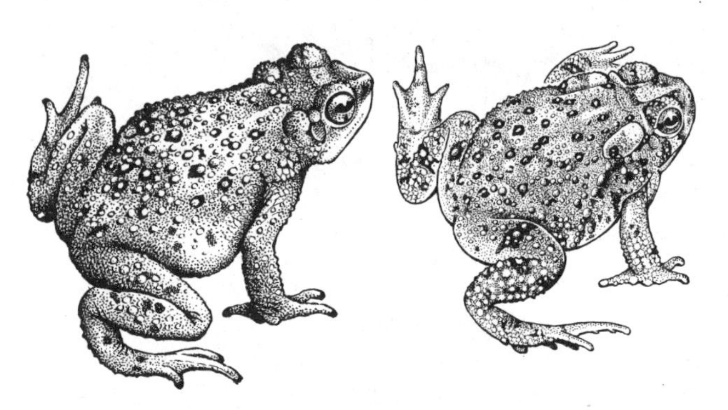

Red-spotted Toad. *Southwestern Toad.*

Southwestern Toad *(Bufo microscaphus)*

Identification: 2–3 in. Above greenish gray to brownish with light stripe across head, including eyelids, and sometimes light patch on each sacral hump and in middle of back; parotoids oval, pale anteriorly; no skin fold on inner side of hind foot; cranial crests weak or absent. Male with pale throat like female. *Habitat:* Washes, streams (sometimes intermittent), and arroyos in semiarid lowlands, hence often called "Arroyo Toad." Frequents sandy banks with willows, cottonwoods, or sycamores. *Range:* Coast Range from near Santa Margarita, San Luis Obispo County, south into Baja California; Transverse Mountains; Mojave River; Colorado River near Needles. Hybridizes with Woodhouse's Toad in tributaries of Colorado River in Nevada, Utah, and Arizona. *Habits:* Chiefly nocturnal but may be active in daytime when breeding; usually moves by hopping rather than walking. Breeds March to July but may be abroad until September. Eggs in tangled jelly strings with single envelope, 1 to 3 eggs in irregular row, usually on bottom in quiet parts of clear streams. Tadpoles match sandy background—olive, gray or tan, mottled with brown; below white; transform at about 1½ inches in total length. Voice a melodious trill lasting 8 to 10 seconds, rising in pitch at first and often ending abruptly; vocal sac round. *Food:* Snails, Jerusalem crickets, beetles, ants, bees, caterpillars, and moths; some cannibalism.

Western Toad *(Bufo boreas)* (Pl. 3)

Identification: 2½–5 in. Above dusky, gray, or greenish with dark blotches; narrow, pale, mid-dorsal stripe; sometimes a light stripe across head including eyelids; weak cranial crests; parotoids variable in shape, usually oval; well developed, sharp-edged skin fold on inner side of hind foot. Young may lack stripe and have bright yellow on underside of feet. *Habitat:* Grassland, woodland, and meadows in forests; gardens, parks, suburbs; breeds in ponds, slowly flowing streams, lakes, canals, and reservoirs. *Range:* Throughout California except desert from Death Valley southward; absent from central high Sierra where Yosemite Toad occurs. Sea level to around 10,000 ft. Coexists and apparently hybridizes with Yosemite Toad at Blue Lakes and perhaps elsewhere in Sierra. Many isolated populations in arid parts of range; Deep Springs Toad, considered by some to be a distinct species, is small, heavily pigmented and isolated at Deep Springs, Inyo County. *Habits:* Nocturnal and diurnal. Found all year except during cold or dry spells. Breeds January to July, later dates at high altitudes. Eggs (Fig. 2), numbering over 16,000 per female, laid in strings in shallow water; 2 jelly envelopes. Tadpoles (Figs. 2, 3) up to 2 inches in total length at time of transformation but often transform at smaller size; above black to olive. Voice, weak chirps; no vocal sac; throat pale in male; female voiceless. *Food:* Insects (grasshoppers, caddisflies, moths, caterpillars, flies, mosquitoes, beetles, bees, wasps, ants), crayfish, sowbugs, snails, and spiders; some cannibalism.

Subspecies *exsul* (Black Toad) of Deep Springs Valley, Inyo County, classed as *Rare.*

Yosemite Toad *(Bufo canorus)*

Identification: 1¾–3 in. Similar to Western Toad but dorsal stripe, when present, a fine hairline; skin smoother; parotoids rounded to irregular, large, flattened and close together; marked sexual differences in color, more so than in Western Toad. Female contrastingly marked with numerous black blotches on olive to gray background; male yellow green to dark olive with spots small and scant; young resemble those of Western Toad. *Habitat:* High mountain meadows and edges of forests; slow streams, snow melt pools and lakes. *Range:* Sierra from vicinity of Kinney Lakes, just north of Ebbetts Pass, Alpine County to Evolution Lake, Fresno County; 6,000 to around 11,000 ft. *Habits:* Diurnal and nocturnal. Active April to October. Breeds mid-May to mid-July. Eggs in irregular beadlike strings and clusters in shallows. Larva resembles Western Toad's but more

Yosemite Toad.

heavily pigmented, has blunter snout and tail tip. Voice a melodious trill of 10 to 20 or more notes in rapid sequence. *Food:* Insects (beetles, ants), centipedes, etc.

Woodhouse's Toad *(Bufo woodhousei)*

Identification: 2–5 in. Resembles Western Toad but above yellowish brown, grayish, or light olive; usually has prominent cranial crests, elongate divergent parotoids, and no sharp-edged fold on inner side hind foot. Male with dark throat. *Habitat:* Grassland, sagebrush flats, mesquite plains, river bottoms, flood plains, woodland, forest clearings, and farmland; soil often sandy. *Range:* Lower Colorado River and irrigated lands of Imperial Valley; orchards near Coachella Canal east of Indio, Riverside County; evidently it has followed canal northward. *Habits:* Chiefly nocturnal. Breeds March to July in shallow sluggish creeks, fresh water pools, and irrigation ditches. Eggs, to over 25,000 per female, laid in strings in tangled mass. Tadpoles resemble Western Toad's but transform under one inch in total length; tail musculature pale below contrasting sharply with remaining dark color. Voice, a nasal "wa-a-a-ah" resembling an infant's cry, lasting 1–3 seconds,

Woodhouse's Toad.

often dropping in pitch at end; vocal sac round. *Food:* Insects (grasshoppers, crickets, moths, caterpillars, flies, beetles, ants, bees, and wasps), sowbugs, scorpions, centipedes, and spiders.

Treefrogs and Relatives (Family Hylidae)

Mostly small, slim-waisted, long-legged frogs, usually with adhesive toepads used in climbing. Toepad anchored to rest of toe by small extra joint which gives toe tip great mobility in climbing. Widely distributed throughout world but greatest number and variety of species in New World tropics.

In tadpoles of California species, oral papillae encircle mouth except for wide gap in center of upper lip; no indentation at sides of mouth (Fig. 3).

Pacific Treefrog *(Hyla regilla)* (Pl. 3)

Identification: ¾–2 in. Occurs in many color forms—green, gray, brown, tan, etc.; can change from dark to light color in few minutes; often has dark spots on back and legs; black eye stripe, that does not change; toepads. Male has dark olive throat. *Habitat:* Varies greatly, from brackish cattail marshes at sea level to mountain meadows above timberline. Frequents ponds, streams, springs, lakes, and reservoirs in open grassland, woodland, or forest and gardens, golf links, and parks in suburban areas. *Range:* Throughout California but absent from desert except along streams (Mojave River), at oases (Pushawalla Palms), and in higher mountains (Panamints); scattered localities along lower Colorado River. To around 11,000 ft. in central Sierra. *Habits:* Nocturnal and diurnal. Good climber but California form usually stays near ground. Breeds January to July, later dates at high altitude; found all year except during cold or dry periods. Eggs (Fig. 2) with 2 jelly envelopes, in loose, irregular clusters attached to vegetation in shallows of ponds, streams, roadside ditches, rain pools, and marshes. Tadpoles (Figs. 2, 3) dusky to olive brown above, eyes set well out at sides of head, as viewed from above, and directed laterally; may reach 1½ inches in total length at transformation. Voice typically a loud two-parted "kreck–ek" with rising inflection, lasting about 1 second; most familiar frog sound in California. *Food:* Insects (leaf-hoppers, spring-tails, flies, stoneflies, ants, wasps, beetles, caterpillars), spiders, isopods, and snails.

California Treefrog *(Hyla cadaverina)*

Identification: 1–2 in. Dorsal surface resembles color and texture of rocks upon which frog normally rests during day—mottled gray and dusky on granite and sand-colored on sandstone (Topanga Canyon); eye-stripe vague or absent; toepads larger and hindfoot webbing greater than in Pacific Treefrog. Male with dusky throat. *Habitat:* Rocky canyon streams and washes where there are quiet pools and some shade. *Range:* South Coast Range from central San Luis Obispo County south into Baja California; Transverse Mountains; Peninsular Ranges; desert oases. Coexists

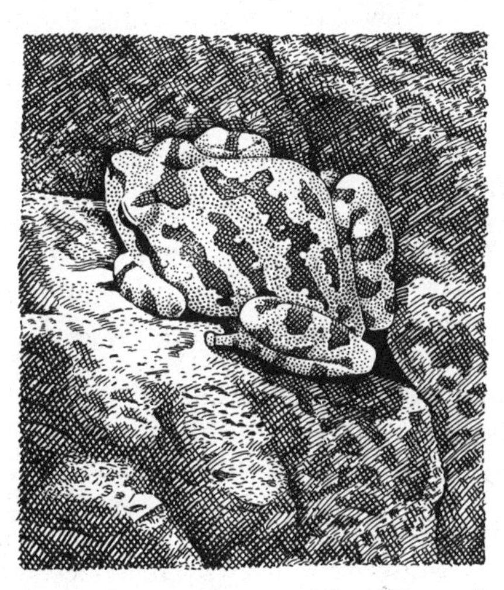

California Treefrog resting camouflaged in a rock cavity.

with Pacific Treefrog at many localities. *Habits:* Nocturnal and diurnal. During breeding season, rests by day in cavities or shallow depressions in rocks, often within one or two jumps of water. When frightened into water, usually quickly seeks shore. Breeds March to May. Eggs (Fig. 2) with single jelly envelope, laid singly, attached to twigs or loose on bottom in quiet water of rocky stream. Tadpoles (Fig. 2) differ from Pacific Treefrog's in having eyes closer together and directed somewhat upward; body more flattened; snout longer; dusky transverse bars on tail musculature; intestines visible through abdominal wall; coloration often blends with sandy, gravelly background. Voice, usually heard at night—ducklike quacks, each call lasting 1/5 to 1/2 second with little or no inflection; vocal sac round. *Food:* Insects (ants, caterpillars, and beetles), spiders, and centipedes.

True Frogs (Family Ranidae)

Almost worldwide in distribution; diverse in form and habits. In New World typically slim-waisted, long-legged, smooth-skinned, anurans with well-developed webbing on hindfeet (Fig. 6i); many have glandular ridge (dorsolateral fold) on upper side extending from eye region to rump; teeth in upper jaw; most are excellent jumpers.

Jelly-coated eggs often laid in globular, grapelike clusters. Tadpoles have oral papillae indented at sides and wide gap across top of upper labium (Fig. 3). Amplexus pectoral.

Red-legged Frog *(Rana aurora)* (Pl. 3)

Identification: 2–5 in. Above brown to reddish (San Francisco Bay region) with small dark flecks and larger blotches; usually with dark mask bordered by pale upper jaw stripe; groin coarsely mottled with black (or dusky) on reddish or yellowish ground color; usually with red (often yellowish in immatures) on lower belly and undersides of legs; well-developed dorsolateral folds. *Habitat:* Found in moist woods, forest clearings, stream border vegetation, and grassland. Seeks quiet permanent water where dense shore growth provides good cover. Frequents ponds, pools along streams, springs, marshes, lakes, and reservoirs. *Range:* North and South Coast Ranges; Transverse Mountains; western slope of Cascade–Sierran Mountain system to southern Sierra; apparently absent from floor of Great Valley. Near sea level to around 4,500 ft. (Sierra). *Habits:* Nocturnal and diurnal. Highly aquatic but less closely confined to water than Cascades and Spotted Frogs. Breeds January to May, later dates to north. Eggs (Fig. 2) in irregular grapelike clusters, 3 to 10 inches in diameter, attached to vegetation in shallows; 3 jelly envelopes. Tadpoles (Figs. 2, 3) yellowish brown above; belly with pinkish iridescence; to around 3 inches at transformation. Voice a stuttering, grating, guttural sound on one pitch often ending in a growl and lasting about 3 seconds; sounds do not carry far; vocal sac expands only slightly; may call from under water. *Food:* Insects (beetles, caterpillars, etc.) and isopods.

Cascades Frog *(Rana cascadae)*

Identification: 1¾–2½ in. Resembles Red-legged Frog but has sharply defined inky black blotches on back and black flecking between blotches scarce or absent; lower belly and undersides of legs yellow; dorsolateral folds present. *Habitat:* Lakes, small streams, and ponds in mountain meadows to near timber line. *Range:* Cascades from Lassen Peak region northward; Trinity Alps. From 3,000 to 9,000 ft. *Habits:* Chiefly diurnal; often basks on water-covered rocks. Highly aquatic; seeks water when frightened but usually escapes by swimming rather than diving. Breeds late May to mid-August. Eggs resemble those of Red-legged Frog but clusters smaller; deposited in exposed shallow water of pools and lake margins. Tadpoles may transform at total length of ¾ inch.

Cascades Frog. *Spotted Frog.*

Spotted Frog *(Rana pretiosa)*

Identification: 2–4 in. Similar to Red-legged Frog but dorsolateral folds less developed, hind limbs shorter, heel (Fig. 6i) usually not reaching to or beyond nostril when leg bent forward along side; eyes turned upward; salmon or yellowish on belly and underside of hind legs, not extending to deeper tissues as in Red-legged Frog; appears painted on. *Habitat:* Frequents springs, small streams, and swamps; low swampy areas in woods and meadows. *Range:* In California known only from Modoc County. *Habits:* Diurnal and nocturnal. Highly aquatic. Time of breeding in California unreported—March to July elsewhere. Eggs in clumps, 3 to 8 inches in diameter, among grasses at edges of ponds; 2 envelopes. Voice a weak, low, clicking sound heard over distance of only about 30 feet (Utah populations). *Food:* Insects (grasshoppers, dragonflies, mayflies, bugs, water striders, aphids, caddisflies, moths, flies, mosquitoes, beetles, ants, wasps), millipedes, centipedes, crayfish, sowbugs, snails, and slugs.

Foothill Yellow-legged Frog *(Rana boylii)* (Pl. 3)

Identification: 1¾–2¾ in. Above gray, brown, reddish, or olive, usually flecked and mottled with dusky; general coloration resembles color of stream bottom with which frog blends; underside of hind limbs and lower belly yellow; triangular light-colored patch on snout; dorsolateral folds indistinct; toe tips usually not dusky. *Habitat:* Rocky woodland and forest streams and rivers with sunny, sandy and rocky banks, deep pools, and shallow riffles. *Range:* Coast Ranges south to Transverse Mountains; throughout northern California to west slope Cascades; south through foothills of Sierra to Tehachapi Creek, Kern County; in region of junction between Cascades and Sierra, ranges far to east along Last Chance Creek near McKessick Peak, Plumas County; isolated populations in southern California in Elizabeth Lake Canyon and drainage of San Gabriel River (near Camp Rincon). To 6,000 ft. in northern Sierra. *Habits:* Chiefly diurnal. Highly aquatic. When frightened dives to stream bottom and hides among rocks or in bottom muck. Breeds mid-March to May when streams subside. Eggs (Fig. 2) in compact grapelike cluster 2–4 inches in diameter, often attached to undersides of stones downstream, in clear, moving water; 3 envelopes. Tadpoles (Fig. 2) mottled, blending with sand and gravel of stream bottom; large mouth and many rows of labial teeth (6/6 or 7/6), somewhat paralleling condition in tail-frog, also a stream dweller; to around 2 inches in total length at transformation. Voice a guttural, grating sound resembling that of Red-legged Frog but rarely heard; throat swells at sides. *Food:* Insects (grasshoppers, hornets, ants, flies, mosquitos, water striders, beetles, moths) and snails.

Mountain Yellow-legged Frog *(Rana muscosa)*

Identification: 2–3¼ in. Above brown with dusky spots; toe tips dusky; undersides of hind limbs, often belly, and sometimes chest, opaque yellow or orange; dorsolateral folds usually indistinct. *Habitat:* Lakes, ponds, and streams in mountain meadows in Sierra and rocky streams in mountains of southern California. *Range:* Through most of Sierra chiefly above 6,000 to over 12,000 ft.; Transverse Mountains and northern Peninsular Ranges in southern California from Pacoima River east and south; 600 to 7,500 ft. Isolated on Mount Palomar. Coexists with Yellow-legged Frog along north Fork of San Gabriel River. *Habits:* Diurnal and nocturnal, chiefly diurnal at high elevations. Highly aquatic; stays near water. When handled smells like garlic. Breeds June to August at high altitudes and March to May when streams subside at lower elevations. Eggs in clumps 1–2 inches in diameter; attached to vegetation or bank in shallows or to rocks in streams; 3 envelopes. Tadpoles have typical tooth formula 2/3 rather than high count of Yellow-legged Frog; may overwinter in Sierra.

Mountain Yellow-Legged Frog. *Leopard Frog.*

Leopard Frog *(Rana pipiens)*

Identification: 2–5 in. Above greenish, light brown, to gray with large dark oval spots, which usually have light borders; well-defined pale dorsolateral folds; white stripe on upper jaw. *Habitat:* Highly varied over total range—from brackish marshes to high mountain meadows and north to tundra ponds. *Range:* In California along Colorado River and San Felipe Creek; irrigated lands of southern Imperial County where it may have come in with irrigation. Introduced at Lake Tahoe, Fallen Leaf Lake, and apparently established along San Joaquin Valley East Side Canal at Yettem, Tulare County and in Bakersfield area. Frogs at Lake City and Alturas, Modoc County, possibly also introduced. *Habits:* Diurnal (often basks) and nocturnal. Attracted to permanent water but may move great distances from water when not breeding. Dives and hides on bottom when frightened. Breeding has been recorded in January along San Felipe Creek. Little known about breeding habits elsewhere. In more arid regions it is opportunistic, ready to spawn whenever it rains. Eggs usually in flattened globular clusters, 3 to 6 inches in diameter, attached to vegetation in shallows of ponds, lake margins, streams, and canals; 2 or 3 envelopes. Tadpoles brownish above, weakly pigmented on belly; intestines visible; to around 3½ inches at transformation. Voice a slow motorboat sound, grunts and chuckles, lasting 1 to 3 seconds; usually calls from surface of water among vegetation, but sometimes from underwater; vocal sacs on each side of neck expand over forelimbs. *Food:* Insects (grasshoppers, crickets, stoneflies, damselflies, mayflies, water striders, back swimmers, caddisflies, caterpillars, flies, mosquitoes, bugs, leaf-hoppers, beetles, ants, bees, wasps), sowbugs, spiders, leeches, small fish, amphibians, small snakes, and birds.

Bullfrog *(Rana catesbeiana)* (Pl. 3)

Identification: 3½–8 in. Above olive or brownish, often grading to light green on head; prominent fold of skin extends from eye around eardrum; no dorsolateral folds; eardrums conspicuous, larger than eye in adult males. Male with yellow throat. *Habitat:* Chiefly lowlands but enters a variety of habitats from grassland to woodland. Frequents marshes, ponds, lakes, streams, and reservoirs. Seeks quiet water where there is plant cover along shore. *Range:* Introduced. Established at several localities in central coastal California by 1922. Now widely distributed throughout most of state. Absent from high mountains and most of desert except in irrigated regions or along water courses (Mojave and Colorado River bottomlands). To around 4,500 ft. in Sierra. *Habits:* Diurnal (often basks) and nocturnal. Highly aquatic; stays near water. Males territorial, floating high in water with yellow throat elevated. Give challenge call on approach of another aggressive high-floating male. Wrestling match may ensue with defeated male, after thrown on his back, swimming away in submissive pose, low in water. Females swim low among males and select mates. Breeds March to July. Eggs in floating mass about 1 egg thick and 1 to 5 ft. in diameter; 10,000 to 20,000 eggs; single envelope. Tadpoles resemble those of Red-legged Frog (Fig. 2), but snout more rounded from above, eyes more widely separated, belly whitish without pinkish iridescence; to 5½ inches in total length at transformation. Voice a low-pitched bellow, "jug-o-rum"; vocal sac single and internal. May squawk when frightened. Tadpoles transform during season eggs are laid (foothills of Sierra) or over-winter. *Food:* Insects (grasshoppers, dragon flies, may-flies, waterstriders, caddisflies, caterpillars, flies, beetles, ants, wasps), small fish, frogs, tadpoles, snakes, turtles, birds, mice; some cannibalism.

Reptiles

LIZARDS

Geckos (Family Gekkonidae)

Tropical or subtropical lizards, usually nocturnal, and with soft skin. Most have toe pads, lidless eyes with vertical pupils, are excellent climbers, and communicate with chirps or squeaks; our only vocal lizards. Our species lay 1 or 2 leathery (Banded Gecko) or hard-shelled (Leaf-toed Gecko) white eggs. *Food:* Insects, spiders, etc.

Leaf-toed Gecko *(Phyllodactylus xanti)*
A crevice dweller that emerges on rock surfaces at night. Adherent toe pads permit it to move rapidly even over undersides of boulders.

Identification: 2–2½ in. Toe tips broad, with pads; skin soft, flexible; eyes large, without movable lids; pupils vertical. *Habitat:* Semidesert mountain slopes; canyons with large rocks. Under rock slabs and occasionally under bark of palo verde, mesquite, etc. *Range:* Lower desert slopes of mountains of southern California—Palm Springs into Baja California. Unreported east of Coachella Valley and Salton Sea.

Leaf-toed Gecko.

Banded Gecko *(Coleonyx variegatus)*
A delicate-appearing, noctural lizard of arid lands often encountered on roadways at night. When first caught, it may squeak.

Identification: 2½–3 in. Skin soft, pliable, with fine granular scalation; pupils vertical; eyelids movable; no toe pads. *Habitat:* Rocky desert flats, washes, and hillsides from pinyon-juniper belt into lowlands; rock outcrops in chaparral areas on coastal side of mountains; sand flats and dunes. *Range:* Desert from Death Valley region south; coastal area, including lower slopes of Peninsular Ranges, from interior Ventura County south; apparently absent from extreme outer coast; foothills of southern Sierra on east side of San Joaquin Valley.

Banded Gecko.

Iguanids (Family Iguanidae)

Chiefly New World lizards of diverse form and habits —terrestrial, rock and sand-dwelling, arboreal, and one species marine (Galápagos Marine Iguana). They include nearly two-thirds of the lizard species in California; all but one (the live-bearing Short-horned Lizard) lay whitish, leathery-shelled eggs that are buried.

Desert Iguana *(Dipsosaurus dorsalis)*
A small desert relative of large iguanas of American tropics. More tolerant of high temperatures than any of our other reptiles, active individuals often with body temperature of 105°F., remaining abroad on hot, sunny

Desert Iguana.

days when other lizards seek shelter. Basks on rocks or sand hummocks, often near burrow in which it may take refuge; climbs bushes to feed on blossoms and to keep cool.

Identification: 4–5½ in. Pale, with gray and reddish brown marks above; round-bodied; tail long; head small, rounded; scales mostly granular on dorsal surfaces; row of slightly enlarged, keeled scales down middle of back. *Habitat:* Creosote bush desert with hummocks of loose sand and patches of firm ground with scattered rocks. Most common in sandy habitats but also occurs in rocky washes, on flood plains, and on clay soils. *Range:* Desert from Panamint and Death Valleys south; range corresponds to that of creosote bush, a staple food. *Food:* Buds, flowers, and leaves of desert plants; occasionally insects and carrion.

Chuckwalla *(Sauromalus obesus)*

Large rock-dwelling herbivore that seeks shelter in rock crevices. When prodded, wedges itself in place by inflating lungs.

Chuckwalla.

Identification: 5½–8 in. Body flattened; loose folds of skin on neck and sides except when inflated; skin sandpaper-like; tail with blunt tip and broad base; rostral scale absent (Fig. 7c), Female and young with crossbands on body and tail. *Habitat:* Restricted to rocky environments—outcrops, lava flows, rocky hillsides, and rocks of alluvial fans. *Range:* Desert from north end of Argus Mountains and Death Valley south; distribution follows creosote bush. *Food:* Leaves, buds, blossoms and fruits of a variety of desert plants including indigo bush, desert mallow, desert tea, burro bush, incense bush, and creosote bush.

Zebra-tailed Lizard *(Callisaurus draconoides)*

Slim long-legged runner capable of speeds up to 18 miles per hour when pursued. Bipedal at high speed. Distracts predators by curling and waving banded tail which if seized can be shed and regrown.

Identification: 2½–3½ in. Body slim; tail long and flat; limbs extremely long and slender; toes lack fringe scales; black crossbars on tail, most prominent on ventral surface ("zebra" markings); pair of black bars in blue area on each side of belly, conspicuous when lizard flattens sides; belly markings faint or absent in female

Zebra-tailed Lizard.

and immatures. *Habitat:* Washes, desert flats of small rocks, hardpan—places where plant growth is scant and there are open areas for running. Occasionally on fine sand but usually not far from firm ground. *Range:* Desert from Saline and Death Valleys south; Cajon and San Jacinto washes on coastal side of mountains. *Food:* Insects, spiders, other lizards, and occasionally blossoms or other plant material.

Fringe-toed Lizards *(Uma)*

Sand-dwellers restricted to fine sand upon which they run with great speed and in which they bury themselves for protection. Highly adapted for sand life—skin of velvet texture reducing friction when burrowing; lower jaw countersunk which prevents sand from getting into mouth; ears protected by ear flaps, eyes by overlapping lids, and respiratory tract by U-shaped nasal passages and nasal valves. Projecting scales form comblike fringe on sides of toes, increasing foot surfaces and aiding locomotion on and within sand. Bury quickly, just beneath surface, vibrating tail to ensure its thorough concealment; they then lie still. Bipedal when running at high speed. Three species, much alike.

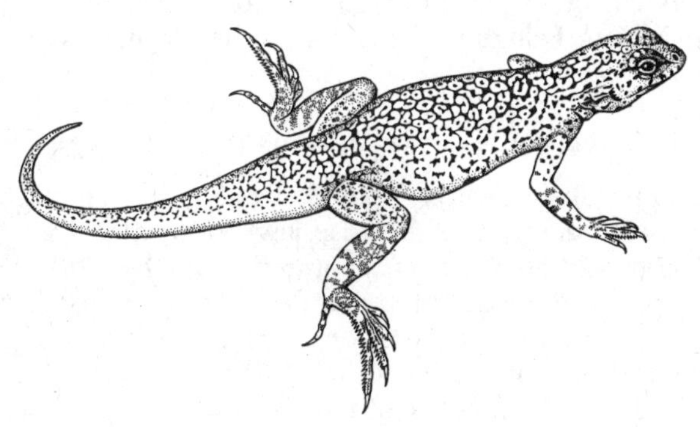

Mojave Fringe-toed Lizard.

Identification: 2¾–4½ in. Body flattened; above with fine granular scalation; toes with fringe scales; sand-matching coloration. *Habitat:* Restricted to fine, loose, windblown sand of dunes and flats. Vegetation usually scant—creosote bush, desert bunch grasses, or other scrubby growth. *Food:* Insects and other arthropods; occasionally buds and leaves.

Mojave Fringe-toed Lizard *(Uma scoparia)*
Black crescents on throat; underside of body pale yellowish green; large black spot and, when breeding, orange patch on each side of belly. *Range:* Mojave Desert.

Colorado Desert Fringe-toed Lizard *(U. notata)*
Diagonal streaks on throat; lacks yellowish green wash; large black spot and, when breeding, bright orange patch on each side of belly. *Range:* Imperial County—Salton Desert west of Salton Sea and Sands Hills south, including lower part of Colorado River Valley, into Mexico.

Coachella Valley Fringe-toed Lizard *(U. inornata)*
Diagonal streaks on throat; black belly spots pin head size or absent (inornate); pinkish wash on sides of belly when breeding. *Range:* Coachella basin from San Gorgonio Pass to near north end Salton Sea. Separated from Mojave Fringe-toe by Little San Bernardino Mountains.

Collared and Leopard Lizards *(Crotaphytus)*

Large, robust lizards capable of overpowering large prey, including other lizards; jaws powerful. Often solitary. Aggressive when captured; hold by sides of head to avoid being bitten and do not cage with other lizards. After mating, females develop orange, or red spots and bars on sides and, in Common Leopard Lizard, orange on underside of tail. Four species, northern Mexico northward, three in California. *Food:* Insects (crickets, cicadas, grasshoppers), spiders, small snakes, other lizards, and ocasionally plant materials. Sometimes cannibalistic.

Collared Lizard *(Crotaphytus collaris)*
Hind limbs powerful and tail long and flattened from side to side. Most abundant where there are rocks for basking, shelter, and lookouts, open areas for running, and adequate warmth. Assumes bipedal locomotion at high speed; tail raised as counterbalance; leaps with agility from rock to rock.

Identification: 3–4½ in. Conspicuous black and white collar; "leopard" spots on face, limbs, and tail; body rounded. Young have broad dark crossbands or rows of dark spots on body and tail; hatchlings with red marks. Breeding female has spots and bars of orange on sides of neck and body. *Habitat:* Rocky canyons, gullies, mountain slopes, and alluvial fans, usually where vegetation is sparse. *Range:* Desert from eastern base of Sierra and mountains of southern California south into Mexico. On coastal side of mountains in headwaters of East Fork of San Gabriel River and San Antonio Canyon, Los Angeles County, and in Cajon Pass area, San Bernardino County.

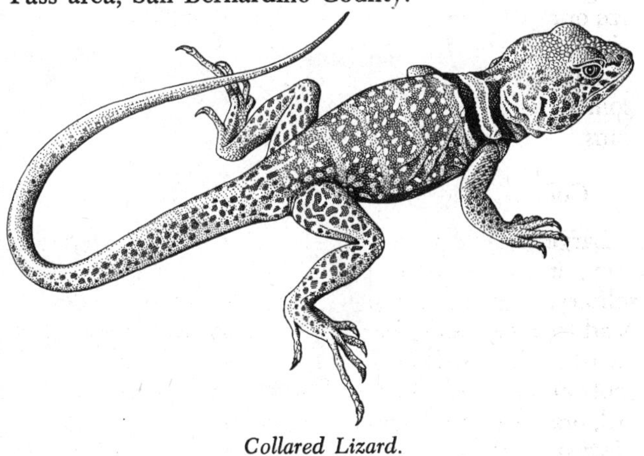

Collared Lizard.

Common Leopard Lizard *(Crotaphytus wislizenii)* Often first seen perched on rock or crouching in pattern of light and shade at edge of bush where its spotted coloration blends. May ambush prey, rushing forth to catch smaller lizards, insects, and other animals that venture near or may cautiously stalk its prey. Avoids dense grass and brush which interfere with running. Bipedal posture at high speed.

Identification: 3½–5 in. Above with "leopard" spots; body round; tail long, round; head large; throat with parallel streaks. In dark phase, spots obscure and light crossbars conspicuous. Reddish markings of breeding female usually in two rows on sides. Hatchlings also have reddish spots. *Habitat:* Arid plains with bunch grass, alkali bush, sagebrush; creosote bush desert; in mountains in pinyon–juniper zone. *Range:* Desert from eastern base of Sierra and from mountains of southern California south. Extends westward from desert to Mount Pinos region where it occurs in isolated populations chiefly in canyons in pinyon–juniper, sagebrush habitat. Has hybridized in past with Blunt-nosed Leopard Lizard; hybrid populations found in Cuyama River

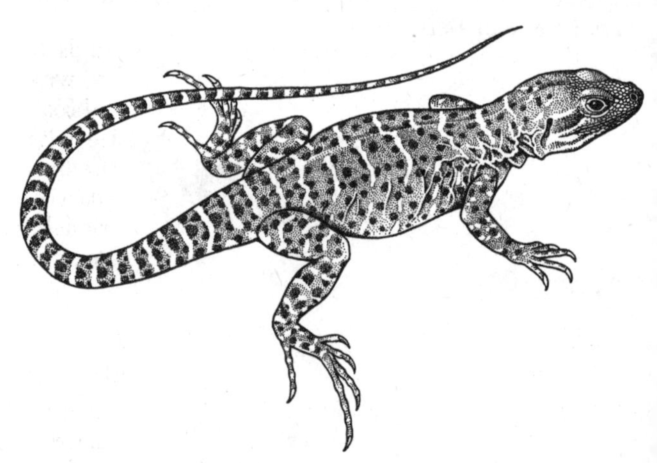

Common Leopard Lizard.

drainage from vicinity of Santa Barbara Canyon to Burges Canyon.

Blunt-nosed Leopard Lizard
(Crotaphytus silus) Endangered species

Identification: Resembles Common Leopard Lizard but snout blunt and throat typically spotted rather than streaked; when streaks present they converge on chin (not parallel as in Common Leopard Lizard). Reddish or orange spots of breeding female in single row. *Habitat:* Barren grassland, often of clump grasses and scattered bushes—iodine bush, saltbush, ephedra. Seeks refuge in burrows of ground squirrels and other mammals. *Range:* San Joaquin Valley and surrounding foothills; Carrizo Plains, southward over Temblor and Caliente Ranges into lower Cuyama Valley. Probably formerly widespread throughout San Joaquin Valley but now over two-thirds of range has been converted to agriculture and species is absent there. In remnants of San Joaquin Desert in Pixley and Kern Wildlife Refuges. From 100 to around 2,000 feet (Carrizo Plain).

Spiny Lizards *(Sceloporus)*

Over 50 species, ranging from tropical lowlands to timberline, Panama to Canada. Males usually with bright blue patch on each side of belly and on throat; blue color reduced or absent in females. Above with projecting keeled, pointed (spiny) scales. Some are live-bearing but all California species lay eggs. *Food:* Insects, spiders, scorpions, centipedes, and occasionally buds and leaves; larger species sometimes eat other smaller lizards; occasionally cannibalistic.

Western Fence Lizard
(Sceloporus occidentalis) (Pl. 4)

Probably best-known California reptile. Lives in a great variety of habitats and has adapted to human habitation, occurring among old lumber piles, about farm buildings, and along backyard fences. Good climber, but in some areas rarely ascends trees.

Identification: 2½–3½ in. Dusky, brown, or gray above with dark blotches; blue patch on throat and on each side of belly, weak or absent in young; females usually lack throat patch and belly patches usually less vivid and smaller than in male; in Sierra (mostly above 7,000 ft.), adults reach large size and big males are nearly solid blue below; underside of forelimbs and back of thighs often yellow; keeled, pointed scales on upper surfaces; complete supraorbital semicircles (Fig. 7c); scales on backs of thighs nearly all keeled (Fig. 7a). *Habitat:* Grassland and woodland, especially where there are rock outcrops, fallen trees, brush heaps, old lumber, or buildings. Avoids dense woods. *Range:* Throughout California except in desert where its distribution is spotty—along river courses and on the higher mountaintops; sea level to over 10,000 feet; Santa Cruz, Santa Rosa, and San Miguel Islands.

Sagebrush Lizard *(Sceloporus graciosus)* (Pl. 4)

Close relative of Western Fence Lizard, with which it coexists at some localities along coast and in the mountains.

Identification: 2–2½ in. Similar to Western Fence Lizard, but scales on back of thighs not keeled (Fig. 7b); smaller dorsal scales; rusty patch usually present on sides behind forelimbs; no orange or yellow on rear of thighs. *Habitat and Range:* Chaparral and open coniferous forests of Cascades, Sierra, and southern California mountains usually in rocky areas above 3,000 feet; scattered populations in canyons of North Coast Range and on mountain tops in South Coast Range (Mount Diablo and Santa Cruz, San Benito, and Santa Lucia Mountains); isolated populations at Sutter Buttes in Sacramento Valley and in desert mountains (Telescope Peak).

Desert Spiny Lizard *(Sceloporus magister)*

Identification: 3½–5½ in. Stocky; large pointed scales on back and sides; above usually yellowish or light brown, with crossbands or spots of dusky, especially in young; dark wedge-shape mark on each side of neck; sometimes broad dark blue stripe on back in male; sides often tinged with yellow or rust; male with blue patch on throat and on each side of belly. Female has orange head when breeding. *Habitat:* Plains and lower slopes of mountains; pinyon-juniper woodland, Joshua tree forest, creosote bush flats, willows and cottonwoods of river bottoms. Frequents rocks and trees where it seeks shelter in rock crevices, beneath bark and fallen branches, and in woodrat nests. *Range:* Inner Coast Range–Panoche Pass, San Benito County, to near Cottonwood Pass, San Luis Obispo County. Throughout desert from north of Mono Lake, southward.

Desert Spiny Lizard.

Granite Spiny Lizard *(Sceloporus orcutti)*

Large, dark-colored, rough-skinned lizard, often seen but extremely wary. Conspicuous when basking on pale-colored rocks. Adults may congregate in deep rock crevices during hibernation and emerge in January and February.

Identification: 3¼–4 in. Close relative of Desert Spiny Lizard but darker, lacks conspicuous neck markings, and has more rounded, less pointed scales; adult male blue below and, in light phase, blue-green above with purple stripe on back. Female with dusky crossbands; no blue or purple markings. Young banded; head rusty. *Habitat:* Rocky areas, frequently near water; vegetation may be oak, chaparral, yellow pine, and, in desert, Washington palms and mesquite. *Range:* Lower slopes of Peninsular Ranges of southern California on both desert and coastal sides from San Gorgonio Pass southward.

Granite Spiny Lizard.

Side-blotched Lizard *(Uta stansburiana)* (Pl. 5)

Most abundant lizard in drier parts of California, but few individuals live more than one or two years. Named for dark spot on side, most conspicuous in males, which may function in species recognition.

Identification: 1¾–3½ in. Scales on upper surfaces mostly granular; dark blotch behind armpit. Males in light phase speckled above with pale blue; female with blotches or stripes, without blue flecks. *Habitat:* Throughout desert from creosote bush flatlands into pinyon-juniper zone of mountains; elsewhere in areas of chaparral, grassland, and open woodland. Common along wash bottoms and on alluvial slopes. *Range:* Throughout California except north coastal region, Sacramento Valley, and Sierra–Cascade Mountains; Santa Cruz, Anacapa, San Clemente, and Catalina Islands. *Food:* Insects, spiders, scorpions.

Long-tailed Brush Lizard *(Urosaurus graciosus)* Arboreal, even sleeping in vegetation on warm nights. Widespread in creosote bushes but found with difficulty because it resembles bark, aligns itself with a branch, and usually remains motionless when approached.

Identification: 1⅞–2¼ in. Tail long and slender, often twice as long as body; above gray, with dusky crossbars; broad band of enlarged scales down middle of back. Male with white-flecked pale blue or greenish patch on each side of belly, lacking in female. Both sexes often with reddish, orange, or yellow throat patch. *Habitat:* Chiefly creosote bush desert, but also frequents bunch grass, trees of washes, streams, and oases, and olive trees, tamarisk, and Washington palms about human habitations. Loose sand usually present. *Range:* Desert from Garlock fault and south end of Death Valley southward. Coexists with Tree Lizard along Colorado River. *Food:* Insects, spiders, and occasionally some plant material.

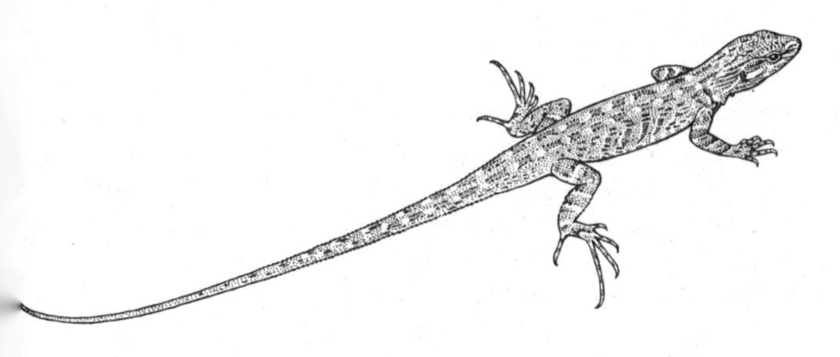

Long-tailed Brush Lizard.

Tree Lizard *(Urosaurus ornatus)*
Climbing lizard that spends much time in trees and on rocks, often clinging head downward. Color usually blends with background. Occupies more humid habitats and is more frequently found on ground and in large trees than Long-tailed Brush Lizard. May congregate in fissures of rocks and trees during hibernation.

Identification: 1⅞–2¼ in. Slim; brown, or gray above with small scales and long slender tail but less than twice length of body; often rust-colored area at base of tail; band of enlarged scales down middle of back, separated into two parallel rows by center strip of small scales. Male with vivid blue or blue-green belly patches, lacking in female; throat blue, yellow, or greenish. Female with whitish, orange, or yellow throat. *Habitat:* open woodland and streamside growth; trees of parks and yards. *Range:* Confined to bottomlands and bordering slopes and tributaries of Colorado River. *Food:* Insects, spiders.

Small-scaled Lizard *(Urosaurus microscutatus)*
Baja California relative of Tree Lizard, barely entering California. Resembles Tree Lizard in appearance and habits.

Identification: 1½–2 in. Above gray, with dark blotches on back; tail less than twice length of body; dorsal scales granular, usually enlarging gradually toward midline. Male with blue throat with center spot of yellow or orange; blue patch on each side of belly. Female lacks blue markings but may have yellow patch on throat. *Habitat:* Bushes and trees of washes, canyon bottoms, and oases, usually in rocky areas. *Range:* Borrego Palm Canyon on desert side and Cottonwood and Deerhorn Flat on coastal side of mountains of southern California, southward. *Food:* Insects, spiders.

Banded Rock Lizard *(Petrosaurus mearnsi)*
A rock-dweller that climbs with ease, limbs sprawled outward and hindquarters swinging from side to side.

Easily moves on sides and under surfaces of boulders. Colors blend with background. Flattened body with low center of gravity aids climbing and sheltering in crevices. Lays 2 to 5 nearly round eggs.

Identification: 2½–3½ in. Flat-bodied: single black collar mark; tail banded; scales on back granular, on limbs and tail keeled (Fig. 7e) and pointed. Male in light phase has blue spots above; female, when breeding, with orange on throat and about eyes. *Habitat:* Confined to rocks, especially larger outcrops, often in shady, narrower parts of canyons on desert slopes of mountains. Inhabits narrow belt between desert lowlands and pine zone. *Range:* San Gorgonio Pass southward on desert side of Peninsular Ranges. *Food:* Insects (including bees), spiders, and buds and blossoms.

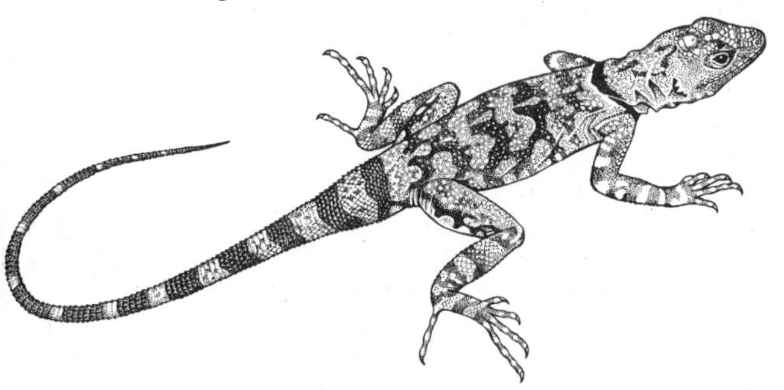

Banded Rock Lizard.

Horned Lizards *(Phrynosoma)*

Readily recognized by prominent head spines, broad flat body, and spiny skin. Some species feed almost exclusively on ants. Their camouflage and spines protect them against predators, especially when they are feeding, and their tough skin and ability to bury in loose soil guards them against attacks of ants. These lizards usually closely match soil color. Dark individuals occur on black lava, nearly white ones on pale sand; others may be pink, gray, or tawny.

When disturbed horned lizards may spurt blood from their eyes, perhaps as a repellent, releasing it from a sinus at the base of the nictitating membrane.

Four California species; three lay eggs; Short-horned Lizard live-bearing. When mating, male may hold female by head spine.

Short-horned Lizard *(Phrynosoma douglassi)*
Cold-adapted species; live-bearing 5 to over 30 young.

Identification: 2½–3¾ in. Short stubby horns; single row of fringe scales on each side of body. *Habitat:* Plains and mountain slopes with sagebrush and other scattered shrubs; pinyon-juniper. *Range*: Eastern Siskiyou and Modoc Counties.

Flat-tailed Horned Lizard *(Phrynosoma mcalli)*
Most often found in vicinity of ant nests and along roadsides where there are sand flats, hummocks, or dunes.

Identification: 2¾–3¼ in. Head spines long and slender; single row of fringe scales on each side of body; dusky stripe down middle of back. *Habitat:* Fine windblown sand of creosote bush and mesquite desert.

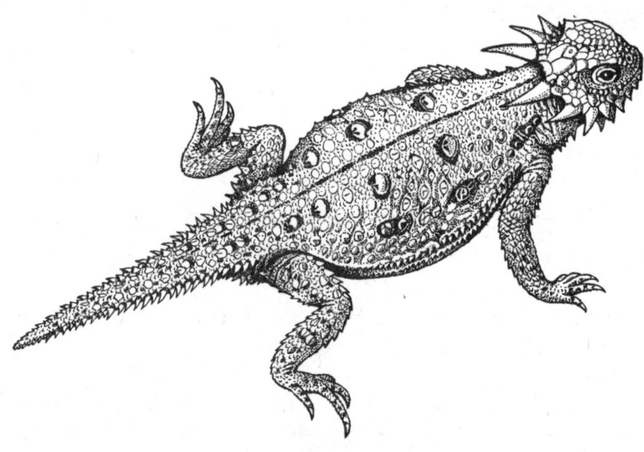

Flat-tailed Horned Lizard.

Range: Coachella Valley southward; flats east of Palm Springs, Riverside County; San Felipe Wash area and Sand Hills, Imperial County.

Desert Horned Lizard *(Phrynosoma platyrhinos)*
Identification: 2¾–3¾ in. Resembles Coast Horned Lizard but snout blunter and horns and body spines shorter; only one row of slightly enlarged scales on each side of throat. *Habitat:* Sandy and gravelly desert where there are scattered bushes and rocks. *Range:* Throughout desert and northeastern part of California along Nevada border; isolated population in San Jacinto River Wash, Riverside County.

Desert Horned Lizard.

Coast Horned Lizard *(Phrynosoma coronatum)* (Pl. 4)
Identification: 2½–4 in. Head and body spines more robust than in other California species; two or more longtitudinal rows of enlarged pointed scales on each side of throat. *Habitat:* Varied. Grassland, brushland, woodland, and open coniferous forest, usually in warmer, drier areas where there is some sand or loose soil. *Range:* From central part of Sacramento Valley southward, including most of Sierran foothills below

4,000 ft., into southern California where it ranges to 6,000 ft. Coast from Sonoma County south; Medicine Lake area, Siskiyou County.

Night Lizards (Family Xantusiidae)

Secretive lizards, that usually shun bright sunlight and, with exception of Island Night Lizard, rarely venture from cover. Small smooth granular scales on dorsal surfaces; large rectangular scales in rows on belly (Fig. 7i). No eyelids; pupils vertical. Live-bearing. *Food:* Insects, spiders, and other arthropods; the Island Night Lizard also eats plants.

Desert Night Lizard *(Xantusia vigilis)*
Prior to the early 1900's, before its yucca habitat was discovered, considered one of rarest reptiles. Once abundant, it is now threatened by land developments and overcollecting which destroy or damage its fragile habitat. Chiefly diurnal and crepuscular. One to 3 young.

Identification: 1½–1¾ in. Olive, gray, or dark brown above speckled with brown or black; eyes without movable lids. *Habitat:* Found under dead yuccas, including fallen branches of Joshua trees, in rock crevices, and, in inner South Coast Range and southern Sierra, beneath logs and under bark of Digger pines. *Range:* Mojave Desert; desert side of Peninsular Ranges southward; inner part of South Coast Range from eastern Santa Barbara County north to Panoche Pass; isolated populations at Granite Station, 1,700 ft., Kern County and San Gabriel Wash, Los Angeles County.

Desert Night Lizard. *Granite Night Lizard.*

Granite Night Lizard *(Xantusia henshawi)*
Concealed by day beneath rock flakes, often on shaded side of boulders. Small size permits it to enter crevices inaccessible to Banded Rock Lizard that shares the habitat. One or 2 young.

Identification: 2–2¾ in. Resembles Desert Night Lizard but head and body flattened and dorsal surfaces with large dark brown or black spots on pale background; pale color becomes reduced to network when lizard in dark phase. *Habitat:* Rocky canyons and hillsides along lower slopes of mountains to about 5,000 feet. *Range:* San Gorgonio Pass southward on desert and coastal sides of Peninsular Ranges into Baja California.

Island Night Lizard *(Klauberina riversiana)*
Much larger and more robust than other California Night Lizards, more likely to expose itself by day and more herbivorous, often about a third of its stomach contents consisting of plant materials. Three to 9 young.

Identification: 2¾–3¾ in. Similar to Desert Night Lizard but larger; two rows of supraoculars (Fig. 7c); above mottled with pale ash gray or beige and yellowish-brown darkened with black; sometimes a pale gray dorsolateral stripe on each side edged with brown and black; occasionally a brown vertebral stripe. *Habitat:* Grassland, clumps of cactus, ice plant, cliffs, and rocky beaches. Secretive, usually hides under objects in daytime. *Range:* San Clemente, Santa Barbara, and San Nicolas Islands off coast of southern California.

Skinks (Family Scincidae)

Most, including California species, are secretive, slim-bodied, short-legged lizards with glossy round-edged (cycloid) scales (Fig. 7g); head often small and neck stout. Numerous species throughout world, many of which have limbs and toes reduced; a few are limbless. Some give birth to their young, but California forms lay eggs. *Food:* Our species eat insects and spiders.

Western Skink *(Eumeces skiltonianus)* (Pl. 5)
Often first detected by rustling sound among dead leaves and glimpse of blue tail as lizard wriggles away rapidly in snakelike fashion. Vivid blue tail of young is thought to divert attack of predators to an expendable part and perhaps to thwart cannibalism by adult males; tail thrashes about when severed (see illus.).

Identification: 2½–3¼ in. Body covered with smooth, shiny scales with rounded even-edged margins; striped pattern at all sizes; tip of tail dull blue or slatey; no longitudinal rows of dark crossbars on back, often present in Gilbert's Skink. Young with vivid blue tail and conspicuous dark and light stripes; dark stripe extends well out on each side of tail (about one-third distance to tip). Orange on face and tail in breeding adult. *Habitat:* Woodland, forests, and grassland, usually where there are rocks, rotting logs, or leaf litter; herbaceous ground cover often present. Throughout northern part of California to Yuba River drainage and lower Sacramento River; coastal mountains and valleys into Baja California; Transverse Mountains; Catalina Island.

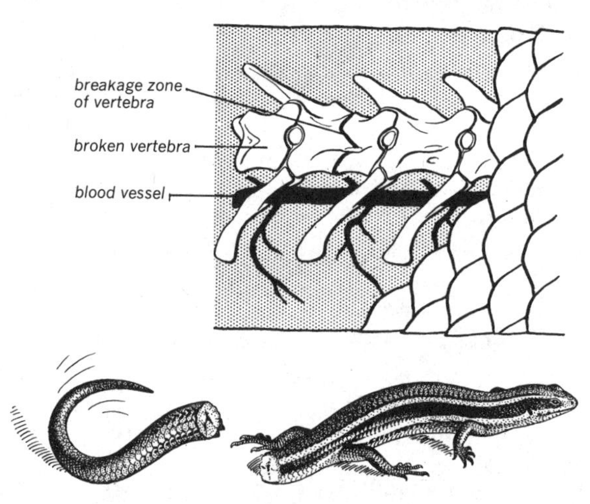

Western Skink shedding its tail.

Coexists with Gilbert's Skink at localities in inner part of South Coast Range and mountains of southern California.

Gilbert's Skink *(Eumeces gilberti)* (Pl. 5)
Color and scale characteristics merge with those of Western Skink at some localities in inner part of South Coast Range, but remain distinct north and south of Yuba River Drainage where the two species meet in the Sierra.

Identification: 2½–4 in. Similar to Western Skink in form and scalation, differing chiefly in color. Large adults usually without stripes, often nearly uniform yellowish or yellow-brown above; usually many dorsal scales have dusky edges; in heavily pigmented individuals markings may form network; lateral stripes, when present, tend to be variegated rather than uniformly brown; no blue tail color in large adults. Young in central Sierra and desert mountains have blue tails, in South Coast Range, pink tails with bluish above, and in southern California pink tails; all differ from young of Western Skink in having dark lateral stripes stopping at base of tail (extending only about ¼ distance to tip). Where the two species overlap and remain distinct, young of Gilbert's Skink have pink tails. *Habitat:* Grassland, woodland, and forest, often in rocky areas near intermittent or permanent streams and springs. *Range:* Scattered localities throughout mountains of southern California but absent from outer coast where habitats are occupied by Western Skink; inner part of South Coast Range; western slope of central Sierra; Tehachapi Mountains; northern San Joaquin Valley; isolated populations on higher mountains in eastern part of desert.

Whiptails and Relatives (Family Teiidae)

Our species are whiptails—slim, long-tailed, active lizards that appear "nervous" and, when foraging, rapidly turn head from side to side, frequently protrude the tongue, and shake their forelimbs as though walking on a hot surface. Scales minutely granular above and large, rectangular and in transverse and longitudinal rows below (Fig. 7i). Head about same width as neck. Egg-laying. *Food:* Insects (termites, grasshoppers, crickets, ant lion larvae, beetles, moths, caterpillars, leaf hoppers, burrowing cockroaches), spiders, other lizards; buried or concealed prey dug up with forefeet. Hidden food evidently detected by odor and tongue–Jacobson's organs mechanism (p. 26).

Western Whiptail *(Cnemidophorus tigris)* (Pl. 4)

Identification: 3–3¾ in. Slim body and long tail, about twice body length; scales above granular, those on belly large and rectangular; striped and barred pattern. Young striped, tail bluish, although not as blue as in young skinks. *Habitat:* Dry environments where there are open areas for running—desert, open chaparral, and drier parts of woodland and forests. Especially common in washes and on sandy and gravelly flats. *Range:* Throughout most of California from below sea level to around 5,000 feet; absent from higher mountains and humid coast.

Orange-throated Whiptail
(Cnemidophorus hyperythrus)

Trim, wary whiptail that forages over large area to obtain termites and other food in its dry habitat. Does not seem to defend territory but postures when another individual approaches its food or water source. When threatening, tips head downward, humps back, stands stiff-legged, elevates base of tail and vibrates its tip. Adults disappear in late July to September, reappearing in spring, but young may be active until December.

Identification: 2¼–3¾ in. Similar to Western Whiptail but adult with more striped pattern; male with pale orange on sides of belly, underside of tail, and on chest; chin and throat orange. Orange in female may be blotchy, pale, and confined to sides of throat, chest, and chin. *Habitat:* Coastal chaparral; washes and other sandy areas where there are rocks and patches of brush; buckwheat, black sage, and chamise are plants often present; soil may be fine and compacted, with scattered sandy patches. *Range:* Laguna Beach, Orange County, and vicinity of Colton, San Bernardino County, west of crest of Peninsular Ranges into Baja California; range overlaps that of Western Whiptail. *Food:* Insects and other arthropods; western subterranean termite, obtained by digging, is staple food.

Alligator Lizards and Relatives (Family Anguidae)

Our species are alligator lizards—body covered with thick, squarish scales (underlaid by bone) in longitudinal and transverse rows (Fig. 7). Strip of granular scales on each side (Fig. 7), in which fold forms allowing movements of otherwise rather rigid body covering. Attracted to intermittent or permanent streams, springs, and seepages where there are rocks, rotting logs, abundant plant growth, and other cover. Although often found on ground, alligator lizards are good climbers and may ascend trees. When first caught they usually attempt to bite and smear their captor with feces. Tail readily lost and severed part thrashes violently. Frequently protrude forked tongue. Sense of smell appears to be well developed, for these lizards can detect concealed food. Three California species; two lay eggs; Northern Alligator Lizard live-bearing.

Southern Alligator Lizard
(Gerrhonotus multicarinatus) (Pl. 6)

Our most arboreal alligator lizard. Climbs to escape predators and to obtain eggs and young of birds. When suspended by its tail it can draw itself up to its support, without help from its limbs, by a pulley-like action of tail. Tip of tail winds around tail base and draws lizard upward; support grasped with hindfeet (see illus.)

Identification: 4–6½ in. Nine or more dusky or brown crossbands between ear openings and line connecting anterior border of thighs; longitudinal stripe or row of dashes down middle of each scale row on belly. Young with broad stripe of tan, beige, or gray, brightening on tail. *Habitat:* Open grassland, woodland and chaparral; borders of forests, but seldom in poorly lighted interiors; in woodpiles, brush heaps, shaded thickets, and under rocks and logs. *Range:* Throughout California but absent from northeastern part, most of desert (found along Mojave River), and apparently from most of San Joaquin Valley except northern part. On western slope of Sierra, in Coast Ranges, and in southern California; east of Sierra near Olancha and Independence, Inyo County; Catalina, San Miguel, Santa Rosa, Santa Cruz, and Anacapa Islands. *Food:* Insects, spiders and their egg cases (including dangerous black widow), snails, eggs, and young of birds, small mammals (young meadow mice).

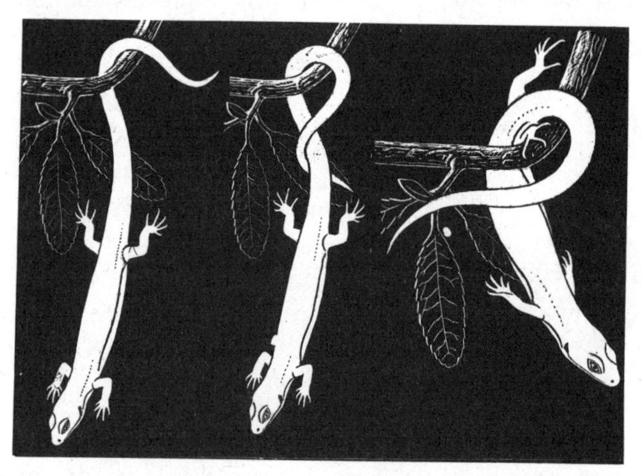

Use of tail in climbing of Southern Alligator Lizard.

Panamint Alligator Lizard *(Gerrhonotus panamintinus)* Secretive species that spends much time in rockslides and dense plant growth.

Identification: 4–6 in. Resembles Southern Alligator Lizard, but generally paler—above light yellow or beige with broad brown crossbands, 8 or fewer, between ear openings and anterior border of thighs; dark ventral markings at middle or sides of scales, forming scattered blotches. Young with contrasting dark crossbars on pale ground color. *Habitat:* Thickets of willow and wild grape near water or in drier habitats grown to creosote bush and desert mint; under rocks and logs on hillsides, in damp gullies, and along streams. *Range:* Known only from Surprise and Hanapauh Canyons, 2,800–4,800 ft., Grapevine Canyon, 4,850–5,100 ft., and Daisy Canyon, 4,000 ft. in, respectively, the Panamint, Nelson, and Inyo Mountains.

Northern Alligator Lizard
(Gerrhonotus coeruleus) (Pl. 6)

Cold-tolerant species that ranges farther north than any other lizard in western North America. Live-bearing; 2–15 (often 6–7) young.

Identification: 3½–5¼ in. Similar to Southern Alligator Lizard but above with irregular dark crossbands or mottled pattern; when present, dark longitudinal lines or dashes on belly are between the scale rows. *Habitat:* Similar to that of Southern Alligator Lizard, but prefers cooler, damper places, with denser plant growth. *Range:* Throughout northern California south in Coast Ranges to northern San Luis Obispo County and in Cascades and Sierra to Kern River; Warner Mountains in extreme northeastern part. In Sierra to 10,500 feet. Range broadly overlaps that of Southern Alligator Lizard. *Food:* Insects, spiders, millipedes, and snails.

California Legless Lizards (Family Anniellidae)

California Legless Lizard *(Anniella pulchra)* (Pl. 5)

Slender, limbless lizard. Burrows in soil sometimes too loose to maintain a burrow. Lacks ear openings; nostrils closed by valves, countersunk lower jaw. Smooth scales offer little resistance to soil and it can readily move backward, aided by blunt tail. In digging, head moved forcefully from side to side by powerful neck muscles, the strength of which can be felt if lizard held by its head. Live-bearing; 1 to 4 young.

Identification: 4½–6½ in. Snakelike, but with movable eyelids and without straplike belly scales found in most snakes; generally silvery above, yellow below; dark individuals along coast from Monterey to Morro Bay. *Habitat:* Loose sand of washes, river banks, and beaches, usually where there are clumps of beach grass, bush lupine, or other scattered shrubs; frequents alluvial soils in oak woodland. *Range:* South Coast Range from Contra Costa County (Antioch) southward; west slope of southern Sierra (to over 6,000 feet) southward, through Tehachapi Mountains west of desert, into Baja California; southern San Joaquin Valley; White Water Wash, Riverside County. *Food:* Insects and their larvae; spiders.

Venomous Lizards (Family Helodermatidae)

Gila Monster *(Heloderma suspectum)*
Large venomous lizard, often slow and awkward but capable of crawling rapidly and lunging suddenly if molested. Venom, produced by glands in lower jaw, flows along grooves in teeth when lizard bites; used in defense and perhaps in subduing prey. Egg-laying.

Identification: 12–16 in. Large and heavy-bodied, with short swollen tail and gaudy pattern of black and pink, orange, or orange-yellow; above with scales resembling beadwork; belly scales squarish. *Habitat:* Lower slopes of mountains and outwash plains; canyon bottoms of arroyos with permanent or intermittent streams; seeks shelter in wood rat nests, dense thickets, and under rocks. *Range:* Eastern slope of Clark Mountains, approximately 7 miles southwest of California–Nevada state line; western base of Providence Mountains, San

Bernardino County; reported at Imperial Dam, Imperial County. Food: Small mammals, eggs of birds and reptiles; lizards.

SNAKES

Blind Snakes *(Family Leptotyphlopidae)*

Western Blind Snake *(Leptotyphlops humilis)*
Slender shape permits entry into ant and termite burrows. Attacks of ants thwarted by covering body with feces and thin clear, viscous fluid from vent which apparently repels ants. Fluids distributed by writhing and moving cloacal region over body coils. Scales elevated giving silvery cast; this perhaps permits fluids to penetrate between them. Slick tough scales protect against abrasion and bites of prey. Under rock flakes that lie flat on ground or against boulders, especially where soil slightly damp. Subterranean; emerges on surface at night or on overcast days. Lays 2–6 elongate eggs.

Identification: 9–16 in. About size and shape of soda straw, with no neck constriction and blunt head and tail; eyes vestigial, appearing as dark spots under head scales; scales shiny and cycloid (Fig. 7g), not enlarged on belly; tail with small terminal spine. *Habitat:* Desert and brush-covered mountain slopes where soil suitable for burrowing and where adequate subsurface moisture. Rocky hillsides with patches of loose soil, and canyon bottoms or washes in vicinity of permanent or intermittent streams. Plants of desert habitats are smoke tree, desert willow, incense bush, ocotillo; those of uplands are white sage, buckwheat, chamise, scrub oak. *Range:* Throughout southern California except in higher mountains from near Point Conception, southern San

Western Blind Snake.

Joaquin Valley and vicinity of Death Valley, southward into Mexico. Many isolated colonies. Sea level to around 5,000 ft. *Food:* Ants and termites.

Boas and Relatives (Family Boidae)

Many are snakes of large size and most occur in warm environments, but our California species are small and the Rubber Boa ranges far north. Above with small smooth scales; pupils vertical. Prey killed by constriction. Primitive traits are paired lungs (most snakes have only one lung) and spurs on each side of vent (best developed in males) which are attached to internal vestiges of hindlimbs and pelvic girdle. In Rosy Boa stroking action of males' spurs on lower back of female causes her to lift her tail and present her vent for copulation. Most boas, including California species, are live-bearing.

Rubber Boa *(Charina bottae)* (Pl. 8)
Crespuscular; occasionally diurnal in spring. Two–8 young.

Identification: 14–30 in. Top of head with large plates; plain brown above, yellow below, without pattern or with a few dusky flecks on lower sides; tail blunt, resembling head, hence called "Two-headed Snake." Young pinkish to light brown above; belly light yellow. *Habitat:* Chiefly a woodland and forest species found buried in sand or loose soil or in and beneath rotting logs, under rocks, and under bark of fallen and standing dead trees. A rocky stream with banks of sand or loam in a coniferous forest with meadows and numerous rotting logs is especially favorable habitat. *Range:* Chiefly a mountain form. Throughout northern part of State in Siskiyous, Cascades, Sierra Nevada, and Coast Range to just north of Point Conception. Farther south known only from Lake Arrowhead and Running Springs, San Bernardino Co., and Fern Valley near Idyllwild, Riverside Co.; reported from 8,500 feet on

Mt. Pinos, Kern Co. Southern form, subspecies *umbratica* (Southern Rubber Boa), classed as *Rare.* Sea level to around 9,000 feet. *Food:* Small mammals (meadow mice, etc.) and lizards.

Rosy Boa *(Lichanura trivirgata)*
Chiefly nocturnal and crepuscular but occasionally abroad in daytime, especially in spring. Six–10 young.

Identification: 24–42 in. Thick-bodied snake with head only little wider than neck; no large plates on top of head or on throat; above slaty, beige, or rosy, with 3 broad brown longitudinal stripes or irregular brown patches; markings sometimes absent; small clawlike spur on each side of vent, most prominent in males. *Habitat:* Rocky brushlands and desert; oases and permanent or intermittent streams but does not require permanent water; washes in rocky canyons. *Range:* Throughout Mojave Desert from Death Valley region (Hanapauh Canyon) to Joshua Tree National Monument, east into Arizona; lower slopes of Peninsular Ranges and Transverse Mountains south into Baja California; along coast from Orange County south; unreported from Coachella Valley southward in low desert. Distribution spotty. Sea level to around 4,500 ft. *Food:* Small mammals and birds.

Rosy Boa.

Colubrids (Family Colubridae)

Most snakes belong to this family. They are highly variable in habits and appearance and worldwide in distribution. Plates on top of head often large and in symmetrical arrangement. Teeth usually solid and similar in size, but some species are venomous and have grooved, enlarged teeth toward back of upper jaw. All California forms are harmless to man.

Ringneck Snake *(Diadophis punctatus)* (Pl. 8)
Seldom encountered in open; usually found under rocks, logs, boards or other objects and when disturbed emits fetid odor and coils tail in tight spiral revealing red ventral color which may warn of unpleasant taste. Sometimes aggregates at favored protected sites which are evidently found and recognized by odor.

Identification: 12–30 in. Slender olive to nearly black snake with dark head and conspicuous yellow or orange neck band; below yellow-orange to red over entire ventral surface, color intensifying on underside of tail; scales smooth (Fig. 7d), usually in 15 rows (sometimes 13) at midbody. *Habitat:* Varied–woodland, forest, grassland, chaparral, farms and gardens; humid environments; in arid regions restricted to mountains and water courses. *Range:* Throughout California except most of floor of Great Valley and east of Cascade–Sierran crest; Catalina Island; isolated desert occurrence in Providence Mountains, San Bernardino County. Distribution spotty. Sea level to around 7,000 ft. *Food:* Salamanders (especially Slender Salamanders), treefrogs, lizards (skinks, etc.), snakes, worms, and insects.

Sharp-tailed Snake *(Contia tenuis)* (Pl. 6)
Feeds on slugs. Has long teeth adapted for holding its slippery food (see illus.). Tail spine, thrust into ground, may help anchor snake when it grapples with prey. Most often found from February through May and in November after rains, when slugs are active. Activity reduced in dry or cold weather. Egg-laying.

Identification: 8–18 in. Above reddish brown or gray usually becoming reddish on upper surface of tail; below with regular, alternating crossbars of black and cream; scales smooth (Fig. 7d); tail with sharp terminal spine. Young red above, fine, dark lines on sides. *Habi-*

tat: Woodland, grasslands, and forest, usually near streams; pastures or open meadows on edges of coniferous forests or among oaks in foothills. Found under logs, bark of standing and fallen trees, rocks, and other objects. Most likely to be found on warm days following rains. *Range:* Siskiyou and Cascade Mountains; west slope of Sierra Nevada; Coast Range from near Eureka, Humboldt County to Pine Mountain, San Luis Obispo County. Distribution spotty. Sea level to 6,600 feet (Mariposa Grove of Big Trees) in Sierra.

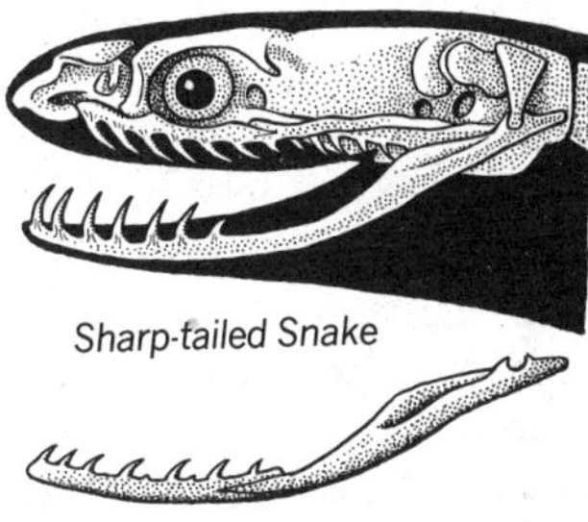

Comparison of tooth length in Sharp-tailed and Ringneck snakes.

Spotted Leaf-nosed Snake *(Phyllorhynchus decurtatus)* Nocturnal, burrowing, egg-laying.

Identification: 12–20 in. Pale, brown-blotched snake with greatly enlarged leaflike scale (rostral) at end of blunt snout; rostral completely separates internasals (Fig. 7c); below white, unmarked; pupils vertical. *Habitat:* Sandy, gravelly washes, alluvial fans, and desert flats. Creosote bush commonly present. *Range:* Throughout desert and on lower mountain slopes along its western boundary. Below sea level to around 3,000 ft. *Food:* Eggs of reptiles.

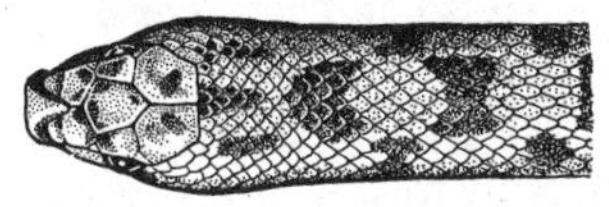 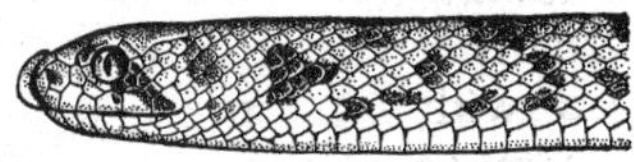

Spotted Leaf-nosed Snake.

Racers and Whipsnakes *(Coluber* and *Masticophis)*

Slim, smooth-scaled, fast-moving, diurnal snakes with large eyes adapted for seeing in bright light. When hunting, head held well above ground and occasionally moved from side to side. Although chiefly terrestrial may ascend bushes and trees. Egg-laying. *Food:* Lizards, snakes, small mammals, frogs, birds and their eggs, insects; and occasionally carrion. Prey ambushed or pursued, seized in jaws, and pinioned under loops of body.

Racer *(Coluber constrictor)* (Pl. 8)
Identification: 22–78 in. Scales in 15 to 17 rows at midbody (15 rows just anterior to vent) (Fig. 7f); plain brown or olive above without markings (except in young); unmarked pale yellow below. Young with brown saddles on back and smaller blotches on sides, fading on tail; faint blotching sometimes still evident in individuals 1½ to 2 ft. long; young resemble small Gopher Snakes from which they can be distinguished by smooth scales (Fig. 7d), large eyes, and wedged preocular (Fig. 7k). *Habitat:* Meadows, open grassland, thin bush, and forest glades, in both semiarid and moist environments but absent from extremely dry areas and high mountains. Attracted to logs, rocks, and other cover. *Range:* Throughout California except desert and parts of San Joaquin Valley; on Santa Cruz Island. Sea level to 6,700 ft.

Coachwhip *(Masticophis flagellum)* (Pl. 6)
When pursued often takes refuge in rodent burrow, among rocks, or in bush where it may defend itself with spirit, hissing and striking repeatedly, and sometimes approaching aggressively. Has been clocked at 8 miles per hour.

Identification: 36–102 in. Our longest snake; scales smooth (Fig. 7d), in 17 rows at midbody (13 or fewer just anterior to vent) (Fig. 7f); no longitudinal stripes;

general tone above tan, gray, or pink with black cross-bars on neck (desert and south of San Joaquin Valley); occasional individuals are black (San Diego County); light yellowish brown or pink without dark head color and neck bands (subspecies illustrated—north of Transverse Mountains); slender body and tail, and scalation suggesting braided whip have given rise to common name. Young blotched or cross-banded with dark brown or black on light brown background; neck markings often faint or absent. *Habitat:* Desert plains, brushland, woodland, and farmland; generally avoids dense vegetation; terrain may be flat or hilly, sandy or rocky; tolerant of dry, warm environments. *Range:* Foothills of eastern Lake County south in Coast Range and San Joaquin Valley through southern California into Baja California; east of Sierra from vicinity of Carson River southward throughout desert; unreported from Sierran highlands and outer coast north of Los Angeles. Below sea level to around 6,000 ft.

Striped Racer *(Masticophis lateralis)* (Pl. 8)

Identification: 30–60 in. Plain black or dark brown above, lightening on tail; conspicuous pale yellow, or cream stripe on each side (orange in coastal mountains east of San Francisco Bay), bordered below by a dark stripe; below cream, becoming coral pink on underside of tail; scales in 17 rows at midbody (Fig. 7f). Easily mistaken for garter snake but lacks median stripe and has smooth scales; coastal form of Western Patch-nosed Snake has enlarged rostral scale. *Habitat:* Chaparral snake; frequents brushlands with scattered grassy patches, and rocky gullies or stream courses; chiefly in foothills but ranges in mountains into mixed deciduous and pine forests. *Range:* From Shasta Reservoir and northern part of Sacramento Valley south along western foothills of Sierra into southern California west of desert; Coast Ranges from Trinity County south; absent from humid northwest coast, most of Great Valley, and desert. Near sea level to 6,000 ft.

Subspecies *euryxanthus* (Alameda Striped Racer), in vicinity of San Francisco Bay, classed as *Rare*. Illustration in Plate 8 is of this subspecies. More typical form has narrower yellow or cream stripes.

Striped Whipsnake *(Masticophis taeniatus)*
An arid lands relative of the Striped Racer.

Identification: 30–72 in. Similar to Striped Racer; black, dark brown, or gray above; whitish lateral stripe on each side, bisected by black line; additional black lines on lower sides; below yellowish, grading to coral pink posteriorly; dorsal scales in 15 rows at midbody (Fig. 7f). *Habitat:* Brushlands, sagebrush flats, pinyon-juniper woodland; attracted to rocky stream courses, permanent and intermittent; in both flatlands and mountains. *Range:* Great Basin east of Cascade–Sierran crest from vicinity of Lava Beds National Monument southward to northern part of Mojave Desert. To 9,400 ft. (Telescope Peak).

Western Patch-nosed Snake *(Salvadora hexalepis)*
Active diurnal racerlike snake capable of great speed even on sand. May be seen hunting for basking lizards during morning hours. Enlarged rostral scale used in burrowing and perhaps in digging up eggs of lizards. Egg-laying.

Identification: 20–45 in. Slender snake, typically with broad yellow or beige dark-bordered longitudinal stripe; large patchlike rostral that fails to separate internasals (see Leaf-nosed Snake) (Fig. 7k); stripe occasionally faint or obscured by crossbands in eastern part of range in Mojave Desert and narrow west of desert; below plain white, sometimes washed with dull orange, especially posteriorly; scales smooth. *Habitat:* Grassland, chaparral, sagebrush plains, and desert scrub; in both sandy and rocky areas on lower slopes of mountains and on low, dry creosote bush plains in extreme parts of desert. *Range:* Southern California north to plains around Shandon, San Luis Obispo County, into southern San Joaquin Valley; in desert to north of Death Valley; vicinity of Wendel, Honey Lake, Lassen County. *Food:* Reptiles and their eggs and small mammals.

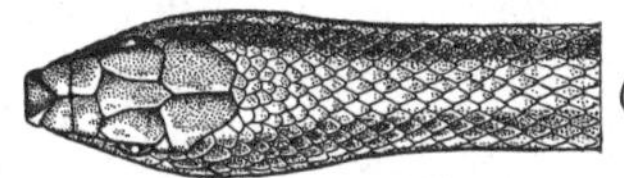 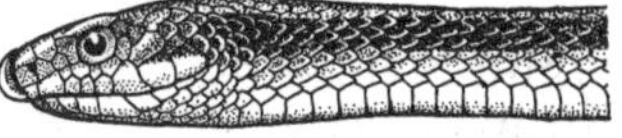

Western Patch-nosed Snake.

Glossy Snake *(Arizona elegans)* (Pl. 6)
Aptly called "Faded Snake" for it often appears bleached. Burrowing snake that emerges onto surface at night. Usually gentle. Egg-laying.

Identification: 27–56 in. Resembles faded Gopher Snake, but scales smooth (Fig. 7d), rather than keeled; lower jaw countersunk; ground color above light brown, gray, pinkish, or cream, blotched with tan or gray, edged with blackish; paler and generally with narrower body blotches in desert than along coast; below unmarked white or pale buff, except for coastal populations, in which edges of ventrals have dark markings. *Habitat:* Chaparral-covered slopes, grassland, light brushy to barren desert, sagebrush flats, and woodland; usually found where there are open areas of loose soil among vegetation. *Range:* Throughout southern California but unreported from coast north of Los Angeles, San Joaquin Valley (except western foothills), and Sierra Nevada; interior South Coast Range north to Mount Diablo. Below sea level to 6,000 ft. *Food:* Lizards, snakes, and small mammals.

Gopher Snake *(Pituophis melanoleucus)* (Pl. 8)
Often mistaken for rattler. Has similar markings and, when alarmed, hisses loudly, flattens and broadens head, and vibrates tail, which among dry leaves suggests sound of rattler. May appear dangerous; actually harmless and beneficial. Good climber and burrower.

Identification: 36–100 in. Ground color yellow or

cream with black, brown, or reddish-brown dorsal blotches (striped individuals sometimes found in Sonoma, Napa and Yolo Counties); smaller blotches on sides; usually dark line across head in front of eyes and from behind eye to angle of jaw; below white to yellowish, often spotted with black; strong contrast in light and dark markings in desert; dorsal scales keeled (Fig. 7e); usually 4 prefrontals (Fig. 7k). Compare with young Racer (p. 118) and Glossy Snake. *Habitat:* Variable. Grassland, brushland, woodland, coniferous forest, farmland, and desert. *Range:* Throughout California except higher mountains; Santa Cruz and Catalina Islands. Sea level to around 9,000 ft. *Food:* Mice, rats, gophers, squirrels, rabbits, birds and their eggs, and lizards.

Kingsnakes *(Lampropeltis)*

Snakes of moderate size, mostly under 5 feet in length, with smooth glossy scales (Fig. 7d); *Lampropeltis* means "shiny-skin." They range from Canada to Ecuador, are egg-laying, and kill their prey by constriction. They have well-developed musk glands which may aid individuals in tracking and recognizing one another. Noted for feeding on rattlesnakes but they do not seek them out in preference to other snakes.

Common Kingsnake *(Lampropeltis getulus)* (Pl. 7) This snake and the Gopher Snake are the most widely distributed snakes in California, occurring in virtually all habitats. Often solitary, only occasionally encountered. Crepuscular and nocturnal in hot weather. Egg-laying.

Identification: 30–82 in. Ringed with plain black or dark brown and white or pale yellow (black and white in desert); pale bands broaden on belly; individuals with more or less continuous pale vertebral stripe or mixed stripe and banded patterns occur chiefly west of desert and south of Transverse Mountains; many of these striped snakes have chocolate brown on belly or on underside of tail; black-bellied individuals with pale crossbands broadening on lower sides to form lateral stripe occur in northern San Joaquin Valley and ones with brown pigment at base of white scales of crossbands in Imperial County; scales smooth and shiny. In Sierra, California Mountain Kingsnake sometimes lacks red markings but white rings usually not broadened on lowermost rows of dorsal scales. *Habitat:* Varied—coniferous forest, woodland, grassland, river bottoms, farmland, chaparral, and desert; found in vicinity of rock outcrops and under rotting logs, old lumber, and rocks. *Range:* Throughout California except higher mountains and extreme northwestern and northeastern parts; Catalina Island. Sea level to 7,000 ft. *Food:* Snakes (many species, including rattlers), lizards, eggs of reptiles and birds, rodents, birds, and frogs.

California Mountain Kingsnake
(Lampropeltis zonata) (Pl. 7)

Also known as Coral Kingsnake and mistaken for the venomous coral snakes although latter do not occur in California. Produces fetid odor when handled.

Identification: 20–40 in. One of our most beautiful snakes; scales smooth, shiny; black, white, and red rings, red bordered on each side with black; red rings may be interrupted on back, appearing as wedge on each side within broad black band, and occasionally, as in central Sierra, may be lacking. *Habitat:* Moist coniferous forest and woodland sometimes mixed with chaparral. Often found in vicinity of rocky streams in wooded areas where there are rotting logs. *Range:* Distribution spotty. Chiefly a mountain form—Siskiyou Mountains, Cascade Range, Sierra Nevada, Coast Ranges, Transverse Mountains, and Peninsular Ranges. Absent from Great Valley and desert. Sea level to 8,000 ft. *Food:* Lizards, snakes, birds (nestlings), and small mammals.

Long-nosed Snake *(Rhinocheilus lecontei)* (Pl. 6) Secretive, nocturnal, crepuscular. Apparently remains underground by day since rarely found beneath objects on surface. Pointed snout and countersunk lower jaw are adaptations for burrowing. Egg-laying.

Identification: 20–42 in. Crossbanded with black and reddish on cream ground color; flecked with white on sides within black bands and with black in interspaces between black bands; below whitish; scales smooth (Fig. 7d), most on underside of tail (caudals) in single row. Speckling on sides faint in young. Banded color phase with wider and fewer black bands, usually lacking red in interspaces, and with scant black spotting on sides, occurs at scattered localities throughout desert and in San Diego County. Single caudals will distinguish such individuals from kingsnakes with which they might be confused. *Habitat:* Desert and brushland; likely to be found on roadways at night in irrigated parts of desert. *Range:* Mendocino and Lake Counties south throughout Great Valley (including adjacent foothills) and southern California; unreported from coast north of Los Angeles except for Palo Colorado Canyon, near Carmel, Monterey County; throughout desert north to northeastern part of State, east of Sierran crest. Sea level to 5,400 ft. *Food:* Lizards and their eggs, mammals (kangaroo rats, mice, etc.), and insects.

Garter Snakes *(Thamnophis)*

Slender snakes with keeled scales and usually striped pattern. Most have a pale stripe down middle of back and one low on each side; color between may be uniform or in blotched or checkered pattern. Stripes afford concealment, especially in grass. Most aquatic of all our snakes, although the more terrestrial species may wander considerable distances from water. Basking frequent in moist surroundings, and all but most southerly form, Checkered Gartersnake, chiefly diurnal. Live-bearing; usually dozen or so young but larger broods have been recorded. When caught usually smear captor with feces and anal scent gland secretions. Species identified with difficulty; note geographic range. *Food:* Fish, frogs, tadpoles, salamanders, earthworms, insects, slugs, small rodents, nestlings and eggs of birds; may scavenge. Prey overpowered (constriction not employed) and swallowed whole.

Common Garter Snake *(Thamnophis sirtalis)* (Pl. 7)

Ranges farther north than any other North American reptile. When cornered often coils, flattens body, displays red markings between scales, and strikes.

Identification: 18–51 in. Dorsal and lateral stripes well defined; red blotches on sides between stripes; top of head olive to black or red; venter bluish gray or dusky posteriorly, becoming pale on throat; eyes large; usually 7 upper labials (Fig. 7k). In San Joaquin Valley and Sierra, ground color slaty or brownish and dorsal stripe broad; in Coast Ranges, color darker, distinct red bars on sides, stripes rather narrow and bright greenish yellow, lateral ones often merging with ventral color; on San Francisco Peninsula, wide dorsal stripe of greenish yellow, top of head red, continuous red stripe on sides. Red markings between stripes, 7 (occasionally 8) upper labials, and large eyes generally will distinguish this species from other garter snakes with which it coexists. *Habitat:* Varied. Ponds, marshes, roadside ditches, streams, sloughs, damp meadows, woods, and farms. Usually found near water which it enters freely. *Range:* Throughout northern California, south along coast to northern San Diego County and to south end San Joaquin Valley and Sierra; absent from desert. Sea level to 8,000 ft. Subspecies *tetrataenia* (San Francisco Garter Snake, Pl. 7e), confined to San Francisco Peninsula, classed as *Endangered.*

Western Terrestrial Garter Snake
(Thamnophis elegans) (Pl. 7)

Identification: 18–42 in. Yellowish or cream stripe down middle of back and cream, whitish or pale gray stripe low on each side; belly color varies but seldom blue; top of head dark; usually 8 upper labials (Fig. 7k). In Sierra, well-defined dorsal and lateral stripes separated by blackish ground color; dorsal stripe yellow or orange-yellow; no red markings; belly pale, unmarked, or with light spotting of dusky coloration. East of Sierra dorsal stripe dull yellow or brown, fading on tail; dark spots on body usually small and well separated but sometimes absent or variously enlarged, occasionally forming black area between stripes. In Coast Ranges dorsal stripe typically bright yellow; bright red or orange flecks usually present on belly and sides, including lateral stripes.

Distinct dorsal stripe and more terrestrial habits usually will distinguish this species in areas of overlap (in Coast Ranges and Sierra) with Western Aquatic Garter Snake. East of Sierra difficulties may be encountered. There Aquatic Garter Snake has narrow dull dorsal stripe ordinarily confined to anterior third of body and checkered pattern of large squarish spots, whereas Terrestrial Garter Snake usually has wider, more fully developed stripe and pattern of rounded, well-separated spots. Along California coast south to northern San Luis Obispo County, where striped variety of Aquatic Garter Snake overlaps range of Terrestrial Garter Snake, former differs in lacking red markings, in usually having orange (rather than yellow) dorsal stripe, yellow (rather than cream) chin and throat, and generally yellow-orange suffusion on ventrals. Northwestern Garter Snake has 17, 17, 15 scale rows (counted respectively on neck, midbody, and just anterior to vent) (Fig. 7f) and 7 upper labials, whereas in area of overlap with Terrestrial Garter Snake latter has 19, 19, 17 or more scale rows and 8 upper labials. Common Garter Snake has larger eyes, generally 7 upper labials, and plain bluish-gray belly; where it coexists with Terrestrial Garter Snake in Coast Range, it usually has greenish-yellow dorsal stripe. *Habitat:* In Sierra and Transverse Mountains, found along streams among bushes or in damp meadows. In Coast Ranges inhabits meadows and clearings with second growth in fog belt, and chaparral. East of Sierra, usually found near streams, pools, and lakes. Permanent water not required; much time spent on land but in drier areas enters water to feed and escape predators. *Range:* Throughout northern California, including Sacramento Valley; Sierra Nevada and region to east; Coast Ranges to Point Conception. Populations in San Bernardino Mountains. Sea level to over 10,000 ft.

Western Aquatic Garter Snake
(Thamnophis couchi) (Pl. 7)

Identification: 18–57 in. Above usually blotched; dorsal stripe often narrow and dull, vague or absent; belly color varies but seldom bluish; top of head dusky; usually 8 upper labials (Fig. 7k); coloration highly variable. In northwestern part and Sierra, gray with conspicuous checkered markings and narrow dull dorsal stripe (confined to anterior part of body in Sierra); below light colored, unmarked, with flesh or purplish tinge toward tail. In San Joaquin Valley size large (to over 4 ft.); dorsal markings of small, well-separated spots in checkered arrangement, dorsal stripe dull yellow, often with irregular margins. In southern part of North Coast Range from Yolla Bolly region and Sonoma County south to San Francisco Bay, yellow to orange dorsal stripe; ground color between it and lateral stripes dark olive to black; throat yellow; belly blotched with gold or pale salmon; iris gray. In South Coast Range to vicinity of San Luis Obispo, dorsal stripe narrower, throat brighter yellow, and iris nearly black. Also in South Coast Range and in Transverse Mountains, Peninsular Ranges, and on Catalina Island, is another variety of this snake, called the Two-Striped Garter

Snake, with dorsal stripe confined to neck, lateral stripes usually present, ground color plain olive or brownish above and dark spots on lower sides; coexists with preceding mid-striped form. *Habitat:* Clear, permanent streams with rocky beds, protected pools, and thickets near shore. In San Joaquin Valley found in streams and sloughs with mud bottoms. Highly aquatic; usually retreats to water when alarmed. *Range:* Throughout California except arid northeastern part and desert. Sea level to 8,000 ft.

Subspecies *gigas* (Giant Garter Snake) of San Joaquin Valley, classed as *Rare.*

Northwestern Garter Snake *(Thamnophis ordinoides)*
Chiefly terrestrial. When alarmed usually retreats to vegetation rather than water.

Identification: 14–37 in. Coloration variable–usually with well-defined dorsal stripe of yellow, orange, or red but stripe may be faint or absent; ground color above black, brown, greenish, or bluish; top of head dark; below yellowish, olive or slate, seldom bluish, often with red blotches; dorsal scales usually in 17, 17, 15 rows (Fig. 7f); typically 7 upper labials (Fig. 7k). *Habitat:* Meadows and clearings in forests where there are clumps of low-growing vegetation. *Range:* Extreme northwestern California, north of Mad River, Humboldt County. Sea level to 4,000 ft.

Checkered Garter Snake *(Thamnophis marcianus)*
Our most southerly Garter Snake; nocturnal on warm nights.

Identification: 18–42 in. Checkered pattern of large squarish blotches on brownish-yellow, brown, or olive ground color; pale yellow vertebral stripe; pair of black blotches at back of head; lateral stripe confined to 3rd scale row (Fig. 7f) anteriorly rather than on 2nd and 3rd scale rows as in our other Garter Snakes. *Habitat:* Grassland, farmland, and stream courses in desert lowlands. *Range:* Colorado River below Parker Dam; irrigated sections of Imperial County and adjacent Mexico.

Western Shovel-nosed Snake *(Chionactis occipitalis)* Adapted for burrowing in sand. Burrows rapidly by lateral movements of shovel-like head. Advancing head is tipped downward at 45° angle creating pocket in sand below snout and throat which makes possible throat movements necessary for breathing. Has smooth scales that offer little resistance to sand, nasal valves, and countersunk lower jaw that excludes sand grains from body openings, angulate abdomen (a longitudinal "ridge" on each side) which reduces lateral slippage when crawling. Emerges to forage at night, after ground surface cools. Occasionally climbs into lower branches of creosote bushes where its banded pattern matches the dark nodes and light-colored internodes of the branches. May sidewind when frightened and moving rapidly.

Identification: 10–17 in. Ground color above yellow or cream, contrastingly marked with black or brown crossbands; may have secondary bands between crossbands–narrow and dark in Death Valley and to east and orange or red south of Mojave Desert; snout shovel-shaped, flatter than in most other snakes; lower jaw countersunk; head little wider than neck. *Habitat:* Restricted to desert; frequents washes, dunes, sandy flats, alluvium, and rocky hillsides where there are sandy gullies or pockets of sand among rocks; vegetation scant. *Range:* Throughout desert from Death Valley into Mexico. Below sea level to around 4,700 ft. *Food:* Insects (including buried larvae), spiders, scorpions, and centipedes.

Western Shovel-nosed Snake.

Western Ground Snake *(Sonora semiannulata)*
Secretive nocturnal relative of Western Shovel-nosed Snake but less well adapted for sand burrowing. Snout less flattened and lower jaw less countersunk.

Identification: 8–19 in. Small, crossbanded, longitudinally striped, or plain-colored snake with head only slightly wider than neck; varied dorsal pattern—dark crossbands may encircle body to form rings, may occur as saddles, be reduced to single neck band, or be entirely lacking; along lower Colorado River has distinct, broad, red or orange median stripe and greenish-gray or bluish gray sides; plain, crossbanded, and striped individuals may occur at same locality; scales smooth (Fig. 7d) glossy. Dark blotch anteriorly on scales distinguishes crossbanded individuals from Western Shovel-nosed Snake. *Habitat:* Similar to that of Western Shovel-nose but less tolerant of extreme aridity. Frequents river bottoms, borders of cultivated fields, desert flats, sand hummocks, and rocky hillsides where there are pockets of loose soil. Along lower Colorado River among thickets of mesquite, arrowweed, and willows. *Range:* Death Valley region east and south along border of State into Mexico. River bottomlands in vicinity of Imperial and Laguna dams, Imperial County. *Food:* Spiders, centipedes, crickets, grasshoppers, and insect larvae.

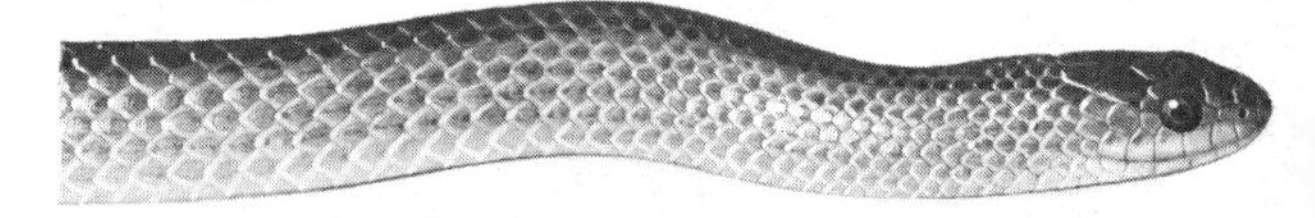

Western Ground Snake.

Western Black-headed Snake
(Tantilla planiceps) (Pl. 6)
Occurs in moist pockets in otherwise arid regions, spending much time underground. Its flattened head suggests that it is a crevice-dweller but little is known about its habits.

Identification: 7–15 in. Small, slender, brown, olive-gray, or tan snake with black head often bordered by narrow white collar; broad salmon stripe down middle of belly; remainder of belly whitish, unmarked; scales smooth (Fig. 7d). On eastern side of San Joaquin Valley, adjoining Sierran foothills, and in desert, dorsal color pale, dark cap usually not extending below corner of mouth, and white collar faint or absent. *Habitat:* Grassland, woodland, chaparral, and desert, under stones on level ground and hillsides. Frequents rocky edges of washes, arroyos, and streams in desert valleys and hills. *Range:* Widespread throughout southern California west of desert but absent from higher mountains; ranges north of Transverse Mountains in inner part of South Coast Range to Sunol, Alameda County; east side of San Joaquin Valley and Sierran foothills to northern Tulare County; scattered localities in desert and its fringes—Saline Valley and Panamint Mountains, Inyo County, and Kingston Range, San Bernardino County; Palm Springs, Snow Creek, Long Canyon, Riverside County; and Mason Valley, Sentenac Canyon, The Narrows, Yaqui Well, San Diego County. Sea level to 6,000 ft. (Sequoia National Park). *Food:* Millipedes, centipedes, spiders, and probably insects.

Lyre Snakes *(Trimorphodon)*

Slender snakes with broad, flat, triangular head bearing a lyre marking; scales smooth (Fig. 7d); large eyes, pupils vertical. Venomous but effect on man little known. Probably not dangerous. Short, grooved fangs toward rear of upper jaw, near level of eyes. Usually must chew to work in venom. Seek mammals (including bats) and lizards in crevices, probably at times when prey inactive. Excellent climbers.

California Lyre Snake *(Trimorphodon vandenburghi)*
Identification: 24–43 in. Twenty-eight to 43 (average 35) brown blotches on back, excluding tail, roughly

hexagonal in shape and split by pale crossbar; ground color above light brown to pale gray; belly cream or pale yellow, often with scattered brown dots; anal single or divided (Fig. 7h, j). *Habitat:* Rock dweller of mesas and lower mountain slopes, often frequenting massive rocks, hiding by day in deep crevices. *Range:* From Ventura County and Tehachapi Mountains, Kern County, south into Baja California, ranging from desert slope of mountains to coast; desert outpost in Funeral Mountains, Inyo County. Sea level to around 3,000 ft.

Sonora Lyre Snake *(Trimorphodon lambda)*
Close relative of California Lyre Snake; may prove to be same species.

Identification: 24–41 in. Thirty-four or less (average around 28) dorsal blotches, excluding tail, and usually divided anal (Fig. 7j). *Habitat:* Desert grassland, wooded bottomlands, rocky canyons, and hillsides. Seldom found in open, rockless or treeless country. *Range:* Eastern part of desert from Ivanpah, San Bernardino County, south into Arizona and Mexico; east of eastern boundary of Joshua Tree National Monument; bottom lands and nearby drainages of Colorado River.

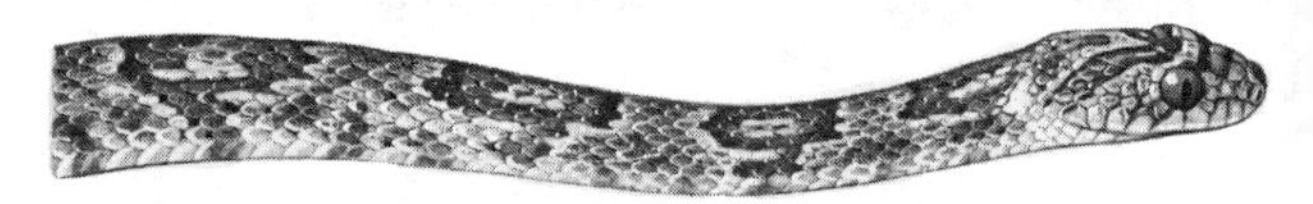

Sonora Lyre Snake.

Night Snake *(Hypsiglena torquata)* (Pl. 6)
Rear-fanged snake that subdues its prey with venom that flows along grooved teeth located toward rear of upper jaw. Secretive, nocturnal, and crepuscular.

Identification: 12–26 in. Gray or beige with dark gray or brown spots and usually two dark brown blotches on neck; blotches may be connected, occasionally absent, and sometimes in group of 3; black or dark brown bar behind eye contrasts with whitish on upper jaw; belly yellowish or white; head flat; pupils vertical; scales smooth (Fig. 7d); anal divided (Fig. 7j). Lyre snakes have lyre-shaped mark on head; Glossy Snake has single anal and rounded pupils; young Racer has round pupils and wedged lower preocular (Fig. 7k). *Habitat:* Plains, chaparral, sagebrush flats, deserts, and woodland from near sea level to lower slopes of mountains; occurs in both rocky and sandy areas. *Range:* Sacramento Valley and adjacent foothills southward; throughout southern California but absent from higher elevations in Sierra, floor of San Joaquin Valley, and extreme outer coast north of northern San Luis Obispo County; throughout desert from north of Death Valley south into Mexico; Santa Cruz Island. Sea level to around 7,000 ft. *Food:* Lizards, salamanders *(Batrachoseps),* small toads, and probably insects.

Rattlesnakes, Vipers, and Relatives (Family Viperidae)

In California this family is represented only by the rattlesnakes. These are heavy-bodied, venomous serpents with a chain of loose-fitting horny segments, the

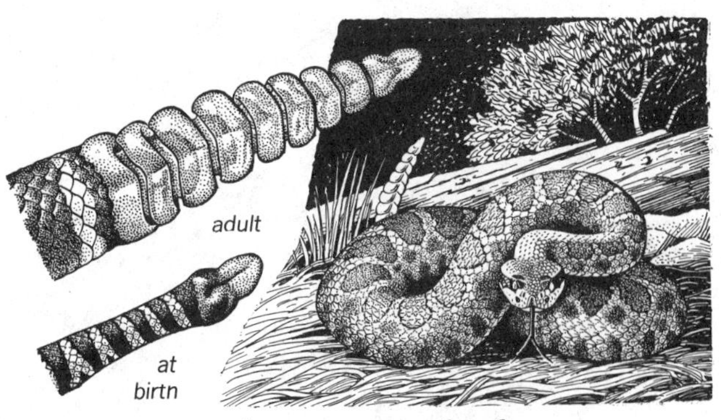

Rattle structure in rattlesnakes.

rattle, at tip of tail, found in no other snakes. Recently born young have blunt, horny button. Triangular head and slender neck; scales keeled (Fig. 7e). Fangs long and hollow, folded back in roof of mouth and covered with fleshy sheath when not in use. Swung outward and exposed during rapid action of strike, carrying venom deeply into tissues of prey. Poison glands located at sides of head behind eyes. Sound of rattle resembles blast of steam and is one of the most startling sounds in nature. Rattle segment added each time snake sheds, from 0 to 6 times a year. Shedding is more frequent in young snakes. Rattle probably evolved to protect these snakes from being trampled by hoofed animals that roamed plains of North America during early stages of rattlesnake evolution.

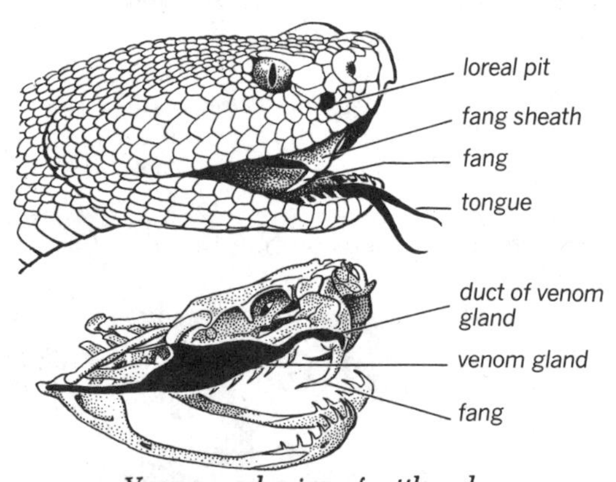

Venom mechanism of rattlesnake.

Prey ambushed and snake usually awaits death of victim before seeking it with help of tongue and Jacobson's Organ—olfactory sense. Loreal pits, temperature sensitive organs, on each side of face between eye and nostril, aid in directing strike. Rattlers usually forage at dusk and at night, but are also abroad in daytime. Live-bearing; most give birth to up to a dozen or so young; Desert Diamondback may have 2 dozen.

Thirty species, Canada to Argentina, swamps to deserts; sea level to around 11,000 feet.

Speckled Rattlesnake *(Crotalus mitchelli)*
Well-camouflaged serpent that blends with its rock or soil background. Watch closely when climbing in its habitat.

Identification: 24–52 in. Color above variable—cream, gray, yellowish, tan, pink, or brown; rough scales and salt-and-pepper speckling suggest granite; markings sometimes vague, usually consist of bands, but may be hexagonal, hourglass- or diamond-shaped; dark rings on tail. Prenasals usually separated from rostral (Fig. 7k) by small scales or supraoculars (Fig. 7k), pitted, creased, or with rough outer edges. *Habitat:* Chiefly a mountain rock-dweller but in coastal southern California it occurs at sea level; frequents barren rocky buttes, open brushland, pinyon-juniper woodland, and occasionally sandy areas. *Range:* Throughout desert, including mountains and adjoining rocky slopes along western border, southern Mono County, south. Peninsular Ranges to coast, south into Baja California; absent from low sandy desert as on floor of Coachella Valley and to south. Sea level to 8,000 ft. (Panamint Mountains). *Food:* Kangaroo rats, mice, ground squirrels, lizards, and birds.

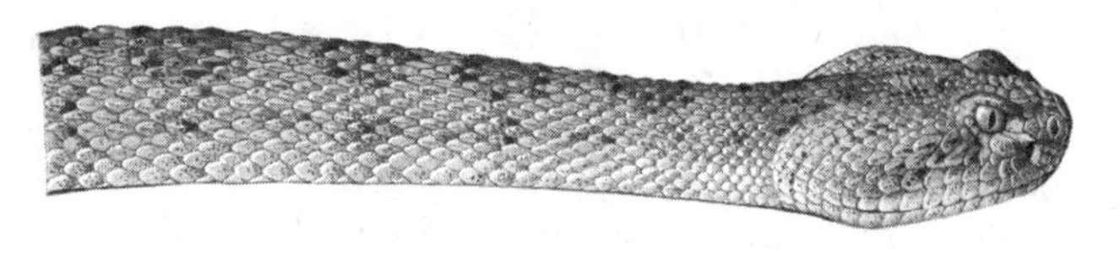

Speckled Rattlesnake.

Western Diamondback Rattlesnake *(Crotalus atrox)*
Spirited snake, often holding ground and vigorously defending itself. Crepuscular, nocturnal, and sometimes diurnal.

Identification: 30–89 in. Largest western rattler; above gray, with brown diamond or hexagonal blotches on back and fainter smaller blotches on sides; markings often indefinite and peppered with small dark spots; tail set off from rest of body by broad black and white rings, about equal in width; light diagonal stripe behind eye intersects upper lip in front of corner of mouth. *Habitat:* Desert plains and alluvial fans with mesquite and other scattered scant vegetation; river bottomlands. *Range:* Throughout low desert south of Little San Bernardino Mountains; absent from Mojave Desert except eastern part where it ranges from near tip of Nevada into eastern portion of Joshua Tree National Monument. Sea level to around 3,000 ft. *Food:* Rabbits, rats, mice, squirrels, birds, and lizards.

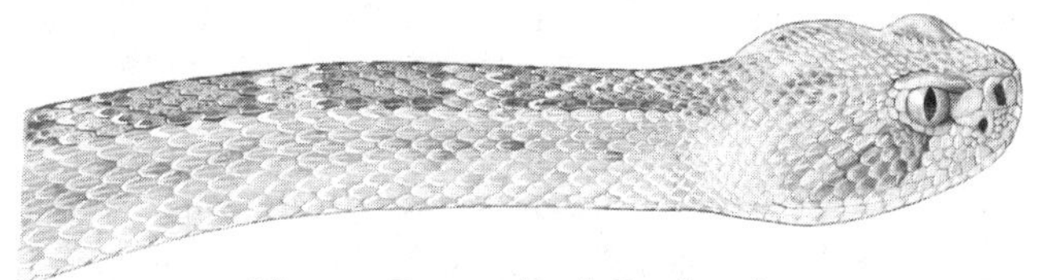

Western Diamondback Rattlesnake.

Red Diamond Rattlesnake *(Crotalus ruber)*
More docile than its relative, the Western Diamondback.

Identification: 30–65 in. Named for its brick red, tan or pinkish coloration; diamond markings usually less well defined and without or with only faint pepper marks; often with white scales between dorsal blotches; tail set off from rest of body by broad black and white rings about equal in width. Young brown or dark gray at birth. *Habitat:* Rocky brushlands on both coastal and desert sides of Peninsular Ranges; also occasionally in grassland and cultivated areas; absent from higher elevations and desert lowlands. *Range:* Peninsular Ranges and adjoining coast from southeastern Los Angeles County and Morongo area, San Bernardino County, into Baja California; almost completely exclusive of and west of range of Western Diamondback. Sea level to 5,000 ft.

Food: Rabbits and rodents (mice, kangaroo rats, ground squirrels).

Red Diamond Rattlesnake.

Western Rattlesnake *(Crotalus viridis)* (Pl. 8)
Identification: 15–62 in. Light stripe behind eye extends behind corner of mouth; dorsal blotches brown or black, usually with light-colored edges giving way posteriorly to crossbands; general coloration variable, but usually harmonizes with predominate soil color—gray, greenish, brown, or black; tail with dark and light rings but not in sharp contrast with body color; usually more than 2 internasals (Fig. 7k), in contact with rostral, a distinctive feature. *Habitat:* Varied—brush-covered coastal sand dunes to timberline; grassland, brushland, woodland, and forest; rock outcrops, talus, rocky stream courses, and ledges; dens in groups in rock crevices or caves in northern part of range and at high altitude. *Range:* Throughout California except desert; Catalina Island. Sea level to around 11,000 ft. *Food:* Squirrels, rabbits, kangaroo rats, gophers, mice, birds, and lizards.

Mojave Rattlesnake *(Crotalus scutulatus)*
Identification: 24–51 in. Well-defined light-edged diamonds or hexagons down middle of back, light scales of pattern usually entirely light-colored; ground color greenish gray, olive-green, or occasionally brownish or yellowish; light stripe from behind eye to corner of mouth; tail with contrasting light and dark rings, dark rings narrower than light ones; enlarged scales on snout and between supraoculars (Fig. 7k). *Habitat:* Barren desert, grassland, and brushland of scattered

scrubby growth such as creosote bush and mesquite. *Range:* Mojave Desert from Death Valley region south to Joshua Tree National Monument. *Food:* Rodents (kangaroo rats) and lizards.

Mojave Rattlesnake.

Sidewinder *(Crotalus cerastes)*
Crawls sideways with body in S-shaped posture. Track distinctive, consisting of J-shaped marks that show impressions of belly scutes. Hook of J points in direction of travel. Sidewinding perhaps evolved to escape predators in open, smooth terrain and on loose fine sand where cover scant and ground has few anchor points for snake's coils. Impressions of belly scutes indicate force is applied chiefly downward and there is little slippage. Hornlike scale (supraocular) above eye (see below) apparently acts as eyelid, folding down over eye, when these snakes encounter rough surfaces (projecting roots, rocks, and gravel) as they crawl through crevices and rodent burrows. Largely nocturnal and crepuscular but occasionally active in daytime or found partly buried in sand at base of bush.

Identification: 17–31 in. Above pale, color harmonizing with background—cream, tan, pink, or gray; brown

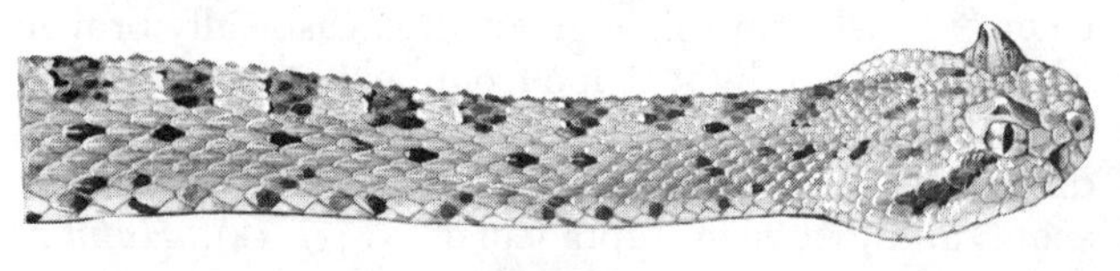

Sidewinder.

blotches on back; supraoculars (Fig. 7k) hornlike, pointed, turned upward, hence called "Horned Rattler." *Habitat:* Chiefly sandy desert, where sand hummocks are topped with creosote bushes, mesquite, or other desert plants, but may occur on windswept flats, barren dunes, hardpan, and rocky hillsides. *Range:* Throughout desert, Mono County southward. Below sea level to 6,000 ft. *Food:* Kangaroo rats, mice, lizards, and occasionally birds.

TURTLES

Water Turtles, Tortoises, and Relatives (Family Testudinidae)

Western Pond Turtle *(Clemmys marmorata)*
Only abundant native aquatic turtle in California. Usually found along streams with deep pools, rocks, and logs that provide basking sites and safe underwater retreats. Usually stays near water, but females travel over land to lay eggs. Active all year in south except during cold weather.

Western Pond Turtle.

Identification: 3½–7in. Shell low, olive, dark brown or blackish, spotted, mottled, or often with dark flecks and lines radiating from center of horny shields that cover shell. *Habitat:* Oak woodland, mixed coniferous and broadleaf forests; grasslands. Quiet waters of ponds, small lakes, streams, marshes, or reservoirs, often where there are rocks, logs, and cattails or other stream border vegetation. *Range:* Throughout California, west of Cascade–Sierran crest; absent from desert except Mojave River drainage; from sea level to around 4,000 feet. *Food:* Aquatic plants, fish, invertebrates, and carrion.

Desert Tortoise *(Gopherus agassizi)*
Its survival is seriously threatened by collecting, highway kills, and disturbance of habitat. Eggs 2 to 9, white, hard-shelled, ping-pong ball size, buried in pit dug with hind limbs.

Identification: 6–14½ in. Shell high-domed usually with prominent growth lines on shields that cover shell; limbs stocky, hind limbs elephantine; tail short. *Hab-*

Desert Tortoise.

itat: Desert oases, riverbanks, washes, dunes, and occasionally rocky slopes. Constructs burrows with half-moon shaped openings, sometimes 20–30 feet long, in northern part of range, often at the base of bushes and in banks of washes. *Range:* Mojave Desert and uplands east of Salton Basin; absent from Coachella Valley. *Food:* Grass, cactus, and other low-growing desert vegetation.

Fully protected from collection, possession, and damage by California State Law. The Texas Tortoise *(Gopherus berlanderi),* although also protected in Texas, is commonly found in pet stores and may have been inadvertently released in our desert along with Desert Tortoises.

Characteristics of Tortoises

Desert Tortoise	Texas Tortoise
Shell usually relatively smooth, to 14½ in. long, elongate from above; nuchal present (small scale at middle of front edge of upper shell).	Shell often with definite bumps, to 8½ in. long, squarish from above; nuchal absent or very small.
Snout rounded	Snout more pointed
Scales on front of forelimb all of nearly uniform size; an enlarged scale near foot on rear of forelimb; smooth scales on elbow.	Forelimb with a few enlarged scales in front, those on rear of nearly uniform size; pointed scales on elbow.
Large spurs on hind limb near foot.	Spurs few and small on hind limb near foot.
Tail not encircled by posterior marginal shields and closely associated upper and lower parts of shell.	Tail almost encircled by posterior marginals and closely associated upper and lower parts of shell.

Mud Turtles and Relatives (Family Chelydridae)

Sonoran Mud Turtle *(Kinosternon sonoriense)*
Highly aquatic. When molested emits fetid odor. Active throughout year but less so in winter.

Identification: 4–6½ in. Head and neck heavily mottled; top of head between eyes flat; shell elongate and high; 9th shield along edge of shell usually no higher than 8th, counting back from front and excluding nuchal, small shield at midline; throat with small nipple-like projections (barbels); tail of male with horny hooked tip. *Habitat:* Woodland ponds, springs, creeks; water holes of rivers and intermittent streams. Prefers mud bottoms. *Range:* Known only from old records along lower Colorado River.

A close relative, the Yellow Mud Turtle *(K. flavescens),* has been reported at Yuma, Arizona, and can be expected in California along lower Colorado River. Similar to Sonoran Mud Turtle in appearance and habits but upper surface of head and neck unmottled, throat pale yellow, low ridge present on each side of head above eye and 9th marginal shield usually distinctly higher than 8th.

Sea Turtles

Large ocean-dwelling turtles, chiefly of tropical and subtropical seas. Low, streamlined shell and large flippers. Come ashore on sandy beaches to lay eggs. Occasionally range northward along California Coast. Most species threatened by commercial exploitation. Flesh and eggs of some highly esteemed.

Green Turtle and Relatives (Family Cheloniidae)

Green Turtle *(Chelonia mydas)*
Named for color of its fat.

Identification: 30–60 in. (120–850 lbs.). Upper surface of shell smooth, with four large shields on each

Green Turtle.

side of shell between row of shields down middle of back and marginals; pair of large scales between eyes. *Range:* World wide in warm seas. Occasional along California coast. *Food:* Eelgrass and seaweed.

Loggerhead *(Caretta caretta)*
Identification: 28–90 in. (to over 900 lbs. but most under 300 lbs). Shell high in front, often reddish brown; five or more shields on each side of shell between row down middle of back and marginals; lacks pair of large scales between eyes. *Range:* Pacific, Atlantic, and Indian Oceans; Mediterranean Sea; southern California coast. *Food:* Crabs, mollusks, sponges, jelly fish, fish, and eelgrass.

Pacific Ridley *(Lepidochelys olivacea)*
Identification: 24–28 (to 80 lbs. or more). Small species; upper shell olive-colored, rather flat-topped, not high in front, with 5 to 9 shields on each side between row down middle of back and marginals. *Range:* Pacific and Indian Oceans. Single record from beach at Table Bluff, Humboldt County. *Food:* Seaweed, mollusks, and sea urchins.

Leatherback Turtles (Family Dermochelyidae)

Leatherback *(Dermochelys coriacea)*
Identification: 48–96 in. (700 to 1,600 or more lbs.). Upper shell leathery, no shields, with prominent longi-

tudinal ridges, dark brown, slaty, or black, sometimes blotched with whitish or cream. *Range:* Worldwide; sometimes encountered far out at sea. Coast of California north to Queen Charlotte Islands, British Columbia. *Food:* Jellyfish and probably other marine animals.

Softshell Turtles (Family Trionychidae)

Spiny Softshell *(Trionyx spiniferus)*
Highly aquatic. Thought to ambush frogs and fish as it lies buried in sand or silt under water, concealed by flattened form and background-matching coloration. Agile, quick-moving, capable of inflicting painful bite; hold by tail at arm's length.

Identification: 3½–17 in. Shell flexible, flattened, covered with leathery skin; limbs flat; toes broadly webbed; flexible proboscis. *Habitat:* Chiefly a river turtle attracted to quiet water with bottom of mud, sand, or gravel, but also enters ponds, lakes, canals, and irrigation ditches. *Range:* Lower Colorado River; irrigation ditches of Imperial County north to Salton Sea. Reported to have been introduced into Colorado River system from New Mexico about turn of century.

INTRODUCED SPECIES

A lively and growing pet trade, use of live amphibians as fish bait, and widespread use of amphibians and reptiles by educational and scientific institutions, is steadily increasing the chances for introductions of non-native species in California. The problem is accentuated by the State's rapid population growth accompanied by a growing demand for pets and great mobility of the human population. All increase the chances of pet dispersal. Most animals released soon die, but there is always the possibility that a colony may become established. Non-native species sometimes thrive at the expense of native ones. Among the amphibians of California, the bullfrog *(Rana catesbeiana)* is a notable

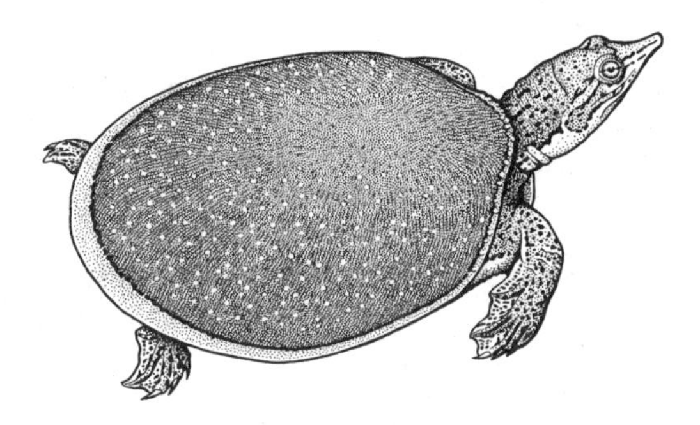

Spiny Softshell.

example. It was introduced into the State as a source of human food after the turn of the century and, aided by commercial frog-farming efforts, became widespread. It now occurs nearly everywhere in suitable habitats except for the desert and higher mountains, and is thought to have contributed to the decline of the native Red-legged Frog *(Rana aurora)* with which it competes. It is now so much a part of the State's fauna, I have included it among the preceding descriptions of native species. The Spiny Softshell Turtle *(Trionyx spiniferus)* is similarly treated because of its long establishment (see p. 144). There are other amphibians and reptiles, however, whose status is less clear. Some may have obtained only a brief toehold and will die out; others, however, may be on their way to establishment. It is important to stop the spread of these exotic animals. They threaten the survival of native species and confuse studies of the natural factors that have given rise to our present fauna.

It is no kindness to a pet to release it in the wild, even in what appears to be favorable habitat. An animal in unfamiliar terrain is almost certain to be killed by predators or die of exposure or starvation. Discarded pets should be given to a scientific or educational institution if they cannot be returned to the place where they were caught.

Introduced species whose status is in doubt are as follows:

African Clawed Frog *(Xenopus laevis)*

Identification: 2–5 in. Smooth skin; rather flattened body; eyes small, on top of head, lidless; large webbed hind feet with several toes armed with sharp black claws.

An African species, commonly used in laboratory studies, and sold as a pet. Highly aquatic. Established in several reservoirs in southern California where reproducing. Young individuals have been found in pools along the Sweetwater River, an intermittent stream below Sweetwater Reservoir, San Diego County.

Snapping Turtle *(Chelydra serpentina)*

Identification: 8–18 in. Chunky head with powerful hooked jaws; lower shell small, only about ⅓ width of upper shell; tail with scales forming saw-tooth crest. Native to central and eastern North America—Canada to Gulf Coast; Atlantic Coast to eastern base of Rocky Mountains. Reported as established in vicinity of Fresno, Fresno County. Feeds on invertebrates, fish, amphibians, reptiles, birds, mammals, and aquatic plants.

Pond Slider *(Pseudemys scripta)*

Identification: 5–14¼ in. Upper shell usually with streaks and bars of yellow on olive or dusky ground color; shell with saw-toothed rear margin; head and limbs striped with yellow; often a broad red stripe or spot (sometimes yellow) behind eye; red-striped individuals called "Red-eared Turtle." Young have green shell; lower shell marked with dark eyelike spots. Common baby turtle of pet shop trade.

Native to central and eastern United States, from southern New Mexico to Atlantic Coast and Michigan to Gulf and into Mexico. Many released in reservoirs, ponds, and lakes in California. Whether reproducing colonies have become established is unknown. Highly aquatic, preferring quiet water with vegetation. Feeds on aquatic plants, snails, tadpoles, and fish.

Texas Tortoise *(Gopherus berlanderi)*

Identification: 5½–8½ in. Resembles Desert Tortoise—see comparison under Desert Tortoise.

Native to southern Texas and northeastern Mexico. Sold in pet shops. Unwanted individuals sometimes released in our desert where they may threaten integrity of the Desert Tortoise. Whether established anywhere, unknown.

Spiny-tailed Iguana *(Ctenosaura hemilopha)*

Identification: 5–10 in. Crest of spines on anterior portion of body; spiny tail; black blotches on back and sides of neck. Young greenish, with ringed tail.

Native to southern Baja California where it frequents trees and rocks. Found in Fullerton, Orange County; some indications that it may be reproducing there.

Blue Spiny Lizard *(Sceloporus cynogenys)*

Identification: 3–5½ in. Spiny scales; broad black collar bordered by white; light spots on neck and back. Male in light phase greenish blue above; throat and belly patches blue. Female gray or brown, also with collar marking.

Native to southern Texas and northeastern Mexico. Sold in pet shops. Free-living individuals have been found at base of Palms to Pines highway, south of Palm Desert, Riverside County. Whether established or not unknown.

CHECKLIST OF CALIFORNIA AMPHIBIANS AND REPTILES

AMPHIBIANS

SALAMANDERS

Ambystomids (Family Ambystomidae)
- Tiger Salamander *(Ambystoma tigrinum)*
- Long-toed Salamander *(A. macrodactylum)* Subspecies *Endangered* (see p. 36)

Northwestern Salamander *(A. gracile)*
Pacific Giant Salamander *(Dicamptodon ensatus)*
Olympic Salamander *(Rhyacotriton olympicus)*

Newts and Relatives (Family Salamandridae)
California Newt *(Taricha torosa)*
Rough-skinned Newt *(T. granulosa)*
Red-bellied Newt *(T. rivularis)*

Lungless Salamanders (Family Plethodontidae)
Del Norte Salamander *(Plethodon elongatus)*
Siskiyou Mountain Salamander *(P. stormi) Rare*
Dunn's Salamander *(P. dunni)*
Ensatina *(Ensatina eschscholtzi)*
California Slender Salamander *(Batrachoseps attenuatus)*
Garden Slender Salamander *(B. major)*
Pacific Slender Salamander *(B. pacificus)*
Kern Canyon Slender Salamander *(B. simatus) Rare*
Tehachapi Slender Salamander *(B. stebbinsi) Rare*
Relictual Slender Salamander *(B. relictus)*
Desert Slender Salamander *(B. aridus) Endangered*
Arboreal Salamander *(Aneides lugubris)*
Clouded Salamander *(A. ferreus)*
Black Salamander *(A. flavipunctatus)*
Mount Lyell Salamander *(Hydromantes platycephalus)*
Limestone Salamander *(H. brunus) Rare*
Shasta Salamander *(H. shastae) Rare*

FROGS AND TOADS

Ascaphids (Family Ascaphidae)
Tailed Frog *(Ascaphus truei)*

Spadefoot Toads (Family Pelobatidae)
Western Spadefoot *(Scaphiopus hammondi)*
Great Basin Spadefoot *(S. intermontanus)*
Couch's Spadefoot *(S. couchi)*

True Toads (Family Bufonidae)
Colorado River Toad *(Bufo alvarius)*
Great Plains Toad *(B. cognatus)*
Red-spotted Toad *(B. punctatus)*
Southwestern Toad *(B. microscaphus)*
Western Toad *(B. boreas)* Subspecies *Rare* (see p. 36)
Yosemite Toad *(B. canorus)*
Woodhouse's Toad *(B. woodhousei)*

Treefrogs and Relatives *(Family Hylidae)*
Pacific Treefrog *(Hyla regilla)*
California Treefrog *(H. cadaverina)*

True Frogs (Family Ranidae)
Red-legged Frog *(Rana aurora)*
Cascades Frog *(R. cascadae)*
Spotted Frog *(R. pretiosa)*
Foothill Yellow-legged Frog *(R. boylii)*
Mountain Yellow-Legged Frog *(R. muscosa)*
Leopard Frog *(R. pipiens)*
Bullfrog *(R. catesbeiana)*

REPTILES

LIZARDS

Geckos (Family Gekkonidae)
Leaf-toed Gecko *(Phyllodactylus xanti)*
Banded Gecko *(Coleonyx variegatus)*

Iguanids (Family Iguanidae)
Desert Iguana *(Dipsosaurus dorsalis)*
Chuckwalla *(Sauromalus obesus)*
Zebra-tailed Lizard *(Callisaurus draconoides)*
Mojave Fringe-toed Lizard *(Uma scorparia)*
Colorado Fringe-toed Lizard *(U. notata)*
Coachella Valley Fringe-toed Lizard *(U. inornata)*
Collared Lizard *(Crotaphytus collaris)*
Common Leopard Lizard *(C. wislizenii)*

Blunt-nosed Leopard Lizard *(C. silus) Endangered*
Western Fence Lizard *(Sceloporus occidentalis)*
Sagebrush Lizard *(S. graciosus)*
Desert Spiny Lizard *(S. magister)*
Granite Spiny Lizard *(S. orcutti)*
Side-blotched Lizard *(Uta stanburiana)*
Long-tailed Brush Lizard *(Urosaurus graciosus)*
Tree Lizard *(U. ornata)*
Small-scaled Lizard *(U. microscutatus)*
Banded Rock Lizard *(Petrosaurus mearnsi)*
Short-horned Lizard *(Phrynosoma douglassi)*
Flat-tailed Horned Lizard *(P. mcalli)*
Desert Horned Lizard *(P. platyrhinos)*
Coast Horned Lizard *(P. coronatum)*

Night Lizards (Family Xantusiidae)
Desert Night Lizard *(Xantusia vigilis)*
Granite Night Lizard *(X. henshawi)*
Island Night Lizard *(Klauberina riversiana)*

Skinks (Family Scincidae)
Western Skink *(Eumeces skiltonianus)*
Gilbert's Skink *(E. gilberti)*

Whiptails and Relatives (Family Teiidae)
Western Whiptail *(Cnemidophorus tigris)*
Orange-throated Whiptail *(C. hyperythrus)*

Alligator Lizards and Relatives *(Family Anguidae)*

Southern Alligator Lizard *(Gerrhonotus multicarinatus)*
Panamint Alligator Lizard *(G. panamintinus)*
Northern Alligator Lizard *(G. coeruleus)*

California Legless Lizards (Family Anneillidae)
California Legless Lizard *(Anniella pulchra)*

Venomous Lizards (Family Helodermatidae)
Gila Monster *(Heloderma suspectum)*

SNAKES

Slender Blind Snakes (Family Leptotyphlopidae)
Western Blind Snake *(Leptotyphlops humilis)*

Boas and Relatives (Family Boidae)
Rubber Boa *(Charina bottae)* Subspecies *Rare* (see p. 36)
Rosy Boa *(Lichanura trivirgata)*

Colubrids (Family Colubridae)
Ringneck Snake *(Diadophis punctatus)*
Sharp-tailed Snake *(Contia tenuis)*
Spotted Leaf-nosed Snake *(Phyllorhynchus decurtatus)*
Racer *(Coluber constrictor)*
Coachwhip *(Masticophis flagellum)*
Striped Racer *(M. lateralis)* Subspecies *Rare* (see p. 36)
Striped Whipsnake *(M. taeniatus)*
Western Patch-nosed Snake *(Salvadora hexalepis)*
Glossy Snake *(Arizona elegans)*
Gopher Snake *(Pituophis melanoleucus)*
Common Kingsnake *(Lampropeltis getulus)*
California Mountain Kingsnake *(L. zonata)*
Long-nosed Snake *(Rhinocheilus lecontei)*
Common Garter Snake *(Thamnophis sirtalis)* Subspecies *Endangered* (see p. 36)
Western Terrestrial Garter Snake *(T. elegans)* Subspecies *Rare* (see p. 36)
Western Aquatic Garter Snake *(T. couchi)*
Northwestern Garter Snake *(T. ordinoides)*
Checkered Garter Snake *(T. marcianus)*
Western Shovel-nosed Snake *(Chionactis occipitalis)*
Western Ground Snake *(Sonora semiannulata)*
Western Black-headed Snake *(Tantilla planiceps)*
California Lyre Snake *(Trimorphodon vandenburghi)*
Sonora Lyre Snake *(T. lambda)*
Night Snake *(Hypsiglena torquata)*

Vipers and Relatives (Family Viperidae)
Speckled Rattlesnake *(Crotalus mitchelli)*
Western Diamondback Rattlesnake *(C. atrox)*
Red Diamond Rattlesnake *(C. ruber)*
Western Rattlesnake *(C. viridis)*
Mojave Rattlesnake *(C. scutulatus)*
Sidewinder *(C. cerastes)*

TURTLES

Water Turtles, Tortoises and Relatives (Family Testudinidae)
Western Pond Turtle *(Clemmys marmorata)*
Desert Tortoise *(Gopherus agassizi) Protected* (see p. 140)

Mud Turtles and Relatives (Family Chelydridae)
Sonoran Mud Turtle *(Kinosternon sonoriense)*
Yellow Mud Turtle *(K. flavescens)*? (see p. 142)

Sea Turtles (Family Cheloniidae)
Green Turtle *(Chelonia mydas)*
Loggerhead *(Caretta caretta)*
Pacific Ridley *(Lepidochelys olivacea)*

Leatherback (Family Dermochelyidae)
Leatherback *(Dermochelys coriacea)*

Softshell Turtles (Family Trionychidae)
Spiny Softshell *(Trionyx spiniferus)*

INTRODUCED SPECIES

Bullfrog *(Rana catesbeiana)* Well established
*African Clawed Frog *(Xenopus laevis)*
*Spiny-tailed Iguana *(Ctenosaura hemilopha)*
*Blue Spiny Lizard *(Sceloporus cynogenys)*
*Snapping Turtle *(Chelydra serpentina)*
*Pond Slider *(Pseudemys scripta)*
*Texas Tortoise *(Gopherus berlanderi)*
Spiny Softshell *(Trionyx spiniferus)* Well established

*Extent to which established unknown